THE
BLESSMAN
APPROACH

THE BLESSMAN APPROACH

by

Lyle L. Blessman

FARNSWORTH PUBLISHING COMPANY, INC.
Rockville Centre, New York 11570

Published by Farnsworth Publishing Co., Inc.
Rockville Centre, New York 11570.
Library of Congress Catalog Card No. 78-64483.
ISBN 0-87863-175-5.
Manufactured in the United States of America.

Dedicated to my wife, Connie ... her support, patience, and understanding from the very first day has given me the pride, confidence, and desire to try to create a better way. Her role as a wife, mother, and good person has given meaningful purpose to whatever success I have enjoyed.

I also want to thank all of those leaders of the Million Dollar Round Table who have created the environment for growing and sharing that is unparalleled in any other industry. The impact these men have had on my life and my life insurance career is immeasurable.

TABLE OF CONTENTS

INTRODUCTION

Over the past ten years I have spent a great deal of time each year away from my office in front of audiences, explaining my philosophy and the methods I use to do business as a life insurance agent. The response I get is heartwarming. Many agents have written to tell me that what I had to say turned their lives completely around. Others said they were on the verge of getting out of the industry because they weren't getting ahead or satisfying the inner need we all have for pride and self-esteem. After applying my methods, they are proud to be agents.

I know very well how they feel. I've been through it myself. The Blessman Approach as it has evolved during my 19 years in the business is a direct outgrowth of that need to make progress, and of that need—perhaps the most important of all—to have the wonderful feeling that comes when you know that through helping others you are helping yourself.

This book is about what I learned, how I learned it, and how I apply it on a day-to-day basis. It has worked well for me and for a host of other agents at varying levels of income and experience. I sincerely hope that what I have to say will be of help and inspiration to you.

Lyle Blessman

1.

GETTING STARTED

I got into the life insurance business—and I'm sure this would apply to most of us—more or less by accident.

When I graduated from Colorado State University there were no recruiters on campus from the big insurance companies extolling the virtues of life underwriting as a career. If there had been I probably wouldn't have listened to them anyway because I was set on becoming a teacher and a coach.

A year later, at the age of 23, having taught biology and assisted the basketball coach at Durango High School in southern Colorado, I decided it was time to take another hard look at my career aspirations and prospects. Some changes were clearly in order. My wife Connie and I were living out of cardboard boxes in a one-room motel apartment. We were expecting a baby, and on the $282 a month I was earning, the outlook was bleak.

After a lot of thought and discussion we concluded we just couldn't make it on that kind of money. I enjoyed teaching, but not enough to starve for it. So I began to look around for another job. But teaching was the only qualification I had. I wondered, what else could I do that would be of value to myself and to others?

It happened that a short time before, my father-in-law had died of a coronary at age 49. I was well acquainted with the great help and solace his life insurance coverage had provided, how vital a role it had played in bringing Connie's mother and the rest of the family through a tragic and difficult period. It seemed to me that certainly here was a real human need, a need I could understand and identify with, something I could see myself becoming a part of. The policy had been written by a Northwestern Mutual agent in Sterling, Colorado, a man who has since retired. I got in touch with him through my mother-in-law and was directed to the Northwestern General Agency in Denver. After some correspondence I was accepted as an agent to work in the Sterling area.

I started out full of energy, pep, ambition, and an enthusiasm that was hard to put down. But it didn't last very long. Looking back on it now, after almost two decades in the business and a measure of success I am proud of, I can honestly say I have never in my life gone through a more discouraging and demoralizing period than my first six months as a Northwestern agent. As the weeks passed by I became more and more deflated. I felt inept and worthless as my self-confidence slowly diminished. It took quite a while for me to believe in myself once again.

*   *   *

When Connie and I—and our cardboard luggage—

arrived in Sterling during June of 1959, we were starting completely from scratch. After having received a week's training in the Denver agency, we headed on up 125 miles or so to the northeastern corner of the state, on the plains that lead gradually up to the Rocky Mountains, to this quiet little farm town on the pretty winding Platte River.

Our assets were meager. After shelling out $104 of my teacher's mustering-out pay for a month's rent on a small house and stocking up a two-week supply of groceries, we had exactly $47 left. By that time our daughter was already three months in this world so that we had a third mouth to feed in the bargain.

But I was optimistic by nature and my hopes for the future were bright. For one thing it gave me satisfaction to note that my draw from the Northwestern was $284 a month, two dollars more than I had been earning as a teacher. That was some kind of progress. Also, even though we didn't know a soul in the whole town of Sterling except for my mother-in-law, I felt at home there right from the outset.

Sterling was a town of 12,000 people, the center of a six to eight county area comprising about 40,000 people, most of whom were in agriculture. I liked that. Having grown up on a farm in central Illinois, I felt at ease in an agricultural setting. I liked the looks of the people, the way they waved and said howdy to each other on the streets, in restaurants and stores. It seemed to me that somehow these were my kind of folks and this was my kind of place. In any case, there I was, more or less in business for myself.

Shoestring Operation

Some business! I didn't have an office. I couldn't

even afford a desk. I worked off the top of a card table in the bedroom. I kept my life insurance applications, medicals, insured savings proposals, insurance forms, and other documents in a carton on the floor because I couldn't afford the price of a briefcase. What I needed with me around town I carried in an old looseleaf notebook. I was operating on a shoestring and one that was rather frayed at that.

The retired Northwestern agent I was replacing in Sterling was very nice to us and tried to be as helpful as possible. But he had no desire to undertake the task of being my instructor. After all, the reason he retired was so that he could take life easy, relax, and enjoy himself. So I was left pretty much on my own.

That was okay with me. I was eager and raring to go, and that's exactly what I started to do. I took off in my car, driving all over the area. I went up to people I had never seen before, introduced myself, and got into conversations with them, getting acquainted, trying to be friendly, talking about everything in the world except life insurance. I avoided this subject for a good reason: I didn't know much about it but was resolved to correct this just as soon as I could. My first objective was to get to know the community and, hopefully, get the community to know me.

Gradually I started to sell by the book because that was the only kind of selling I knew about. I made package presentations, doing the best that I could with what little information I had. I made a real Eagle Boy Scout attempt. I made day calls and night calls and studied every spare minute I had. Adhering religiously to the company's standard training program, I kept meticulous records to keep track of the progress I made.

Earning a living selling insurance, or selling

anything else, is no lark. I was aware of this from the outset. But that didn't bother me. I was prepared to work hard and was seeking no easy road. Having grown up on a farm, I understood the meaning of hard work—and the joys it can bring. So I kept plugging away. The idea of quitting never entered my head. That was one thing I had learned from my father. Nonetheless, geared up though I was, I was in no way prepared for the deep-down feeling of discouragement and the gradual erosion of self-confidence that began stirring in me, a feeling that would continue to grow and overwhelm me as I made my daily rounds through the town and surrounding areas.

Who Needs It?

Looking back now over the years I can easily see how my demoralization was inevitable. I was a salesman without a real market. Or without a real market I knew about at the time.

Every salesman knows the power of enthusiasm. We've all had it drummed into us often enough. But as far as I'm concerned, you can take the most gung ho salesman in the world, and if he hasn't zeroed in on a market for his products, if he doesn't find potential customers who need what he has to offer, he won't make it in the marketplace.

That's the position I found myself in when I started my career as a life insurance agent in Sterling. In my week of training in Denver I had been told that my first customers probably would be people my own age and income level. This was the market I went after at the outset. I might as well have been selling skis in an old age home.

The people I talked with were mainly in their early

twenties. They were milk delivery men, carry-out clerks at the market, service station attendants. Most of them had one or two children just as I did. Their incomes ranged around $300 a month and they were having a rough time of it, just as I was. Oh, they were friendly and sympathetic enough. They wished me all the luck in the world. But there wasn't a thing they could do to improve it. Living from hand to mouth, just as I was, they had little if any money to set aside for life insurance or anything else.

That wasn't the half of it. It took very little time for me to find out I wasn't the only life insurance agent in town. Far from it. Just about every one of those young people I was calling on with my canned presentations already had been called on over and over again by most of the 25 other agents in town. That's right, 25! Quite literally, that's how many there were. So I discovered very early in my career that all of those young people my own age, people starting out in life without any money or immediate prospects of getting any, were about as hard to sell as I myself would have been. I was getting turndowns all over the place. And it was then that my hopes and enthusiasm started to waver.

Call Reluctance

If a sequel to "Death of a Salesman" is ever written, an apt title might be "Call Reluctance." When an agent starts dreading the calls he has to make, he's in for serious trouble.

During that first summer of 1959, the more calls I made and the more rejections and brush-offs I experienced, the stronger the feeling of call reluctance became ingrained in me. Very often I would get into my car and drive out to visit one of the farm families outside of town. Then, after having driven 20 or 30 miles to see

them, I would turn down the lane leading to the farmhouse and, seeing someone there, would lose my nerve. I
would go all clammy and sweaty, back out to the
highway, drive somewhere and park. Then I'd get out of
the car and sit up on the hood, scared to death to go back
there and face those people.

When you talk about call reluctance I understand
the meaning of that term inside out, upside down, and
backwards. Brother, I have been there and back. I
couldn't tell you how many times I went through that
procedure, sitting there for hours on end bawling myself
out, butterflies in my stomach, listening to the radio,
feeling guilty as hell, but unable to get my act back
together, unable to pump myself up. Sometimes it would
take two or three false starts before I could actually
work up the courage to make that approach. All kinds of
apprehensions would be flashing through my mind.
What if I got a rude rejection? What if I was embarrassed, or made to feel like a fool? The situation pro-
gressed from bad to worse to desperate. I lived in mortal
fear of being shown up or put down, insulted or hurt.

When nighttime came I would drive home dejected-
ly, unable to level with either my wife or myself. Connie
would ask me how my day went and I'd say fine. I was
too embarrassed to reveal my true feelings. I was
ashamed of my inadequacies, and didn't want to face up
to them. Another time later on perhaps I would work up
the courage through sheer force of will to drive out there
again, go right up to the farmhouse, get out and make
myself do it. But each time I experienced call reluctance,
the next time became a little harder to live with.

The Dawn's Early Light

After a few months of this, fortunately, a faint glim-
mer of light started to dawn. All of this time, don't

forget, I had been working and studying hard, learning more and more about the insurance business, hammering away at the company's training program, listening to tapes, devouring articles and books, listening to whatever information and advice I could get from knowledgeable people and from some who weren't so knowledgeable. And through it all I was observing the methods of the established veteran life insurance salesmen, agents who supposedly knew the business and all the tricks of the trade.

Well, the more I observed, the less impressed I became. I realized you don't give people real service by using "tricks of the trade." One thing that began getting me down was the package presentation approach. Most agents seemed to be using it and for me, it wasn't getting results, and for another, it wasn't professional. Somehow or other it seemed to me life insurance agents weren't getting the same kind of respect folks in other occupations—banking, the law, accounting—appeared to command. I found this depressing. If you're to succeed in any profession, I thought, respect was absolutely essential—self-respect and the respect of others.

Another thing that bothered me was the hit and run philosophy I too often observed. An agent would sell someone a $5,000 or $10,000 policy, and that's the last the client would see of him for years.

Finally, and what really started getting to me, was the realization that trying to do business with people my own age who simply didn't have the money for the product I was trying to sell them was like batting my head up against a concrete abutment. The market simply wasn't there. Competing with 25 other agents for $5,000 and $10,000 policies the buyers couldn't afford began to strike me as something unreal and ridiculous. I could see myself winding up stuck in the same financial bind I had experienced as a teacher.

Nor was I alone in my reasoning. I had become friendly with a very successful druggist who ran a thriving pharmacy on Main Street. An outspoken man, one day he put the proposition to me blindly. The summer was drawing to an end and he had been watching me run myself ragged day in and day out to very little avail, writing very few policies.

"Well, son," he said, "isn't it about time you went back to teaching? Hasn't it occurred to you yet that you're not going to make it in the insurance business? Look at all these young fellows making the rounds week after week; they don't make it either. They last a year or two, then go on to something else. Smarten up, son, you were trained to be a teacher. *That's* what you ought to be doing."

Well, I realized two things then and there. First, however tough it had been, however hopeless the outlook, the idea of quitting had never occurred to me. I guess it wasn't part of my nature.

The other thing, equally important, was that this astute businessman knew what he was talking about. He was right. I *wouldn't* make it in the insurance business if I continued on the course I was following, making mindless package presentations to people who couldn't afford what I was presenting to them. So, while on the one hand I had no thoughts of quitting, on the other I realized I would have to change my approach, alter my style and philosophy.

The idea kept nagging away at me. There had to be a better way to build my career in life insurance. Somehow or other I had to develop an approach that was unique and professional, one that would allow me to respect myself and make others respect me. This was an absolute must, I decided. If I couldn't develop myself into a respected professional in the industry, if I couldn't find some way to make a real and positive contribution, I wanted no part of the business.

I told the druggist I had no intention of quitting. "But I'm going to find a better way," I said. "I'm going to change my approach. I don't know how I will do it. But I'm going to do something unique."

The Blessman Approach

Right then I started designing what is now sometimes referred to as The Blessman System or Approach. I had no clear idea at the outset where I was heading or what I wanted to do. But I was beginning to get a pretty good idea of what I *didn't* want to do. I wanted no part of the traditional, high pressure approach. I didn't want to operate like the much publicized insurance agent who uses gimmicks and trickery.

You've seen Mr. Average Agent in action. He's read all that stuff about the law of averages being on your side if you make enough tries. If Jones doesn't go for the bait, he reasons, he'll simply move on to the next guy. Enough moves, enough bites.

Part of this image and approach, I suppose, is the fault of the industry. It's true that from what I have seen sales training today is becoming a bit more sophisticated, but it's been pretty poor up to now. And trainees are still being lured by the numbers game. You take a list of 30 prospects and if you get to see 20 out of the 30, and if nine or ten give you facts, the law of averages will be on your side, and so on and so forth.

The novice agent has been trained to go out with his rate book and applications and concentrate on what is really a very narrow segment of the market, not zero in on the client's real and specialized needs. Actually, he's not trained to see the whole picture, and he's not disciplined to roll up his sleeves and work his head off. This is one of the most important things that I learned early on, that seeing the whole picture and hard work go together. When you apply yourself you learn where you're at.

I speak from long hard personal experience. I've had dozens of agents tell me during those first two or three years, "Hey, kid, you're dumb, you're running yourself into the ground. I've already landed a ten and a couple of fives early this week; I've got another ten coming through. I already made my two hundred. You'll be knocking yourself out on that guy for another 30 days and you probably won't sell him. Take a tip from an old pro. I'm taking it easy the rest of the week, going fishing, playing golf. Wise up, kid, it doesn't pay to knock yourself out."

The hell it doesn't. That philosophy may be all right for some, but it's not the one I was looking for.

So I kept plugging along, fumbling, groping, looking for some way that was different. Then one day I started calling on men who were older and wiser than myself. I started calling on men who were successful. If nothing else this was a change. And before long I discovered that successful people were only too happy to give you their time if you approached them in the right way, with humility and sincerity. If they saw you were a young fellow who wanted to learn, they respected you for it and were eager to help.

I asked them all kinds of questions. What made you successful? What do you think about the insurance industry and about people who sell insurance? Well, friendly and communicative as they were, I was surprised to learn that they all felt the same way about insurance, that it was a necessary evil. And as far as the insurance agent was concerned, well, he didn't rank very high in their estimation. He wasn't considered a professional in the same way a lawyer, accountant, or banker is considered a professional.

In any case, the more I probed, the more I learned. And gradually the realization came crashing down on me. These men, however smart and successful and sophisticated they might be where their own businesses were concerned, had very little knowledge or understanding about insurance. And most of them had no idea at all how they could use insurance as a financial and management tool. Despite all the high paid advice and counsel they got, nobody had ever talked to them about insurance, its applications and uses, and how it could most effectively be tied into their businesses and estates.

Their attorneys discussed legal matters and drew up legal documents. Their accountants worked up the statements and saw that their books were in order. Their bankers gave them advice about banking. But all their agents ever did were to sell them policies. No clear definition of overall objectives and needs, no discussion about how insurance can and should work into the overall financial and capital structure. All I saw was a great empty void. Where insurance was concerned, these bright, sharp, savvy entrepreneurs had never been educated. What about those 25 other agents? Most of them hadn't even been there. Most of them steered clear of businessmen who were successful because they were self conscious and uncomfortable in their presence.

It was a startling revelation. And it has since been confirmed year after year, wherever I travel to speak. On platforms from California to Maine, I hear the same thing repeated. Very few agents call on these people. Nobody sits down with them to explain how insurance fits into the overall picture, or how their very real and pressing needs can be met.

The Emerging Plan

Well, perhaps you can see where I was heading. I was just beginning to see it myself.

I kept probing and learning and as I did so, my purpose and direction began to take shape. Here, all over the place, were rich and successful businessmen with net worths of a quarter of a million dollars, a half million dollars, and more. They were getting legal advice, accounting advice, advice from their bankers. But nobody, and certainly no insurance agent, was helping them or working with them to coordinate the whole financial plan of their enterprise. Yet whatever they did—their buying and selling, capital planning, accounting, and production, all their legal transactions—was interrelated and should have been tied together, with their insurance coverage a vital piece of the whole. And nobody was sitting down with them to coordinate these activities. It was costing them thousands of dollars in the near term and over the long pull jeopardizing the holdings they had worked so hard to accumulate.

Here at last, I thought, was a vital need that was simply crying to be filled, an opportunity to perform a real and valued service, and Lyle Blessman, I decided, was just the guy to fill it.

But it wouldn't be easy. Hard as I had worked and plugged those past few months, I would have to work even harder in the months to come. I would have to dig even deeper. I would have to take people apart, to find out what made them tick. I would have to study their business and understand their problems and needs almost as well as they understood them themselves. At the same time I would have to deepen my expertise about the insurance industry, about The Northwestern and the products it offered, about all the most current laws, rulings, and provisions with regard to the applications of insurance.

Finally, and this was the ultimate objective, I would have to design a program specifically tailored to the client's problems and needs. And I would have to do this with the cooperation and assistance of his attorney, accountant, and banker. In short, I would play the role of financial advisor and coordinator.

A tall order indeed. But as I already mentioned, the hard work didn't faze me. I'm the kind of person who thrives on hard work. Hard work charges my batteries.

Another plus in my favor is that I have this great faith in American free enterprise and in the power of positive thinking. I believe that people are basically honest and decent, that if you respond to them positively they will respond the same way to you, and that if you build a better mousetrap and convince them it is better they sure as sunrise will beat a path to your door. Well, that was my intention precisely, to build a better mousetrap, to design a financial program that would so clearly and undeniably be of value to these people they couldn't afford to reject it. If I focused exclusively on this goal, I decided, making service my primary objective and credo, forgetting what might be in it for me, I had faith that Lyle Blessman would somehow be taken care of in the process. And I never regretted that decision.

You know, one thing most successful people I have met have in common is that, having worked hard to achieve what they did, they have a deep and healthy respect for hard work and for people who are willing to dig in. That put me at a remarkable advantage over most other agents right from the start. I knew a mountain of work was confronting me. And I knew nine out of ten agents would walk away from that mountain and say, "No, sir, that isn't for me!"

Most people in my experience tend to shy away from the tough chores, from the study and digging, from the unpleasant tasks. It calls to mind a story I once heard about John Brody, the 49ers' superstar quarterback. He was asked one day, "You're nationally acknowledged as one of the great quarterbacks in the game. You have great hands, a great arm, a keen mind. You pick those defenses apart every Sunday and win so many ball games. Why is it that someone of your stature has to hold the ball for the place kicker to kick that extra point?"

Well, John Brody thought for a moment and frowned slightly. Then he said, "Well, hell, if I didn't hold that ball, it would fall over."

What I'm trying to say is that so often the really successful person is the one who performs the simple troublesome chores the unsuccessful person doesn't like to do and balks against doing. I think what makes the big difference in this business we're in is getting back to the basics, taking care of the blocking and tackling, and holding that ball for the place kicker to kick.

There's a Job To Be Done

So there I was with a long range plan forming in my mind and a tough job cut out for me, first to educate myself about my clients and the industry, then to educate the client. I'm not talking now about the struggling, hand-to-mouth guy who couldn't afford to buy what I was selling, but the rich and successful businessman who I could see desperately needed what I could give him, and in most cases needed it in a hurry before tax complications got too far out of hand, but didn't really understand his own need or how the product could help him.

You know, throughout the years I couldn't tell you how many times I've had life insurance agents come up and tell me about this big fantastic deal they were working on, the close all but cinched, when the deal was killed by the prospective client's accountant or lawyer. Or the banker advised the client against it. Well, I submit that the problem doesn't lie with the attorney, accountant, or banker. It lies with *us*! We're the life insurance experts. It's our job to put our products across. But you can't do it by rote. You can't do it with canned presentations. You have to educate these people. You can't assume that their lawyers, accountants, and bankers are telling them all they need to know.

They're not. The lawyer talks law. The accountant talks accounting. The banker talks about money. But nobody is explaining to the client how all of these things mesh and interrelate, how with insurance included they can all be linked together to produce a strong financial structure. What I am saying is that no one is on hand to coordinate his financial activities. In a nutshell, that's the job I set out to do. And I realized early in the game that there was only one way to do it: not by *competing* with the lawyer, accountant, and banker, not by *downgrading* these professionals, but by working with them to get their support and approval and to win the cooperation I would need to do the best job for the client.

I am talking about a real, honest-to-goodness, marketplace need, the kind whose fulfillment constitutes valuable and genuine service, which is at the root of good professional salesmanship.

I can testify from long personal experience that the market is there in abundance. The demand for your product is there because three out of four of this nation's rich and successful businessmen are operating with that need unfulfilled. They're not getting the information they ought to be getting. And they're not being sold the insurance products they need to protect their assets and serve them when tragedy strikes.

There is enough of a market for all of us. Thousands of successful businessmen throughout these great 50 states need and are not getting the kind of coverage you have to offer them. Thousands need to be educated as to how insurance can most appropriately, *on a carefully individualized basis,* fit into their long range financial plan. It is a vast and rich market that is largely untapped, and it is waiting for the right agent with the right philosophy and approach who is dedicated to helping and serving his clients. These people desperately need personalized expert attention, and I can tell you they will be only too happy to pay for it if they get it.

There are countless thousands of people the life insurance industry still hasn't reached. I have been reaching my fair share of them for more than 19 years now, and I like to think I have been giving them what they need. They have been giving me what *I* need in return, and I'm not talking about money alone. I'm talking about self-respect, self-satisfaction, and pride. When these arrive the money comes as a byproduct.

In those early days, I had no clear idea of where I was heading or where I would ultimately wind up. I knew for certain what I *didn't want to do;* and I saw the vague shape of what I would like to accomplish beginning to form. Right then I began designing what is now The Blessman Approach. For the next three years I studied, planned, and with the help of experience, developed the system, the alternative I was seeking, my own way, the *better* way.

From talking with thousands of agents over the past decade or more, I know there are many, perhaps the majority, who have gone through and are going through, what I experienced during those early months in Sterling. I know there are some who are doing well but can't see any progress ahead. If you are one of this number—starting out and distressed by what you have been running into, or established and stuck at a certain plateau—I offer you what I have learned and derived from my experience.

I found a better way for myself, a way that has been rich and rewarding. Hopefully, with the help of this book, you will find a better way too.

2.

YOU CAN DO IT TOO

However vague and uncertain my direction at the outset, the day I started searching for a different way to sell life insurance—a way I could call my own—things began to look up.

Actually, "up" was the only way I could go. During those first six months I kept carefully documented records. They showed I had made 857 calls and had been rejected 832 times. That's a lot of rejection. The 25 sales I made amounted to a total volume of $174,000. A rather dismal performance.

Deciding to put the past behind me, I continued to make call after call, visiting scores of successful, prosperous farmers, ranchers, and businessmen in the area who were admired and respected.

I'm not knocking it, but I never cared for sitting at my desk on the telephone. And I'm not much of a letter writer. I would rather jump into my car and get moving. And this I did day after day. I'd approach a man on his farm or ranch, in his machine shop or car dealership, stick out my hand and say, "I'm Lyle Blessman of the Northwestern Mutual. I just stopped by to meet you."

I was intrigued by his business and told him so. No longer was I pushing and hustling, obsessed by the compulsion to make a sale and write up that policy. Then all at once something interesting happened. My call reluctance vanished completely. It just seemed to dissolve. I was no longer "selling." I was probing and learning. I was only 23 years old at the time, and most of the people I visited were in their forties and fifties, well fixed and capable, owning a good deal of property. Yet I had no inhibitions about introducing myself because I found out right from the outset that the age difference was unimportant to them. They simply shook my hand, sized me up, and said they were pleased to meet me. I was welcomed wherever I went.

When I asked these men for information and advice, they candidly answered my questions. I was equally candid. I said, "Look, I'm young and I'm lacking in experience. There's a lot I don't know." They asked, "What are you looking for? What do you *want* to know?"

I told them I wanted to know what made them successful, how they operated their business, what it took to be successful in business.

They responded as if I was their son. They told me what I wanted to know and I took it all in and digested it. They explained to me what doing business was all about. I learned about banking and money, about supply and demand, about customer relations. They told me some of the mistakes they had made when they were young like myself, and mistakes they had seen others make.

I wanted to know what was important to them and this I heard wherever I went. Honor! They stressed the importance of being trustworthy and truthful, of keeping your word when you give it. They stressed something else, too: the importance of identifying and fulfilling needs. If you can help a person solve a problem or give him something he needs, he will be only too glad to do business with you. As an equal, not as a favor, you take *his* problem and make it *your* problem and the chemistry begins.

I was just beginning to learn in those days that whatever you sell, whether it's life insurance or bridges, the sale is secondary. The idea is to fulfill the need. The rest will take care of itself.

Well, there I was. To a man they told me I should take the time to get to know people, find out what their plans and goals are, what's important to them, what they want to accomplish. If you want to deal with a businessman, find out what he wants for himself and his family. Hunt and dig for the facts. Take nothing for granted.

Talk with enough people, I discovered, and you can find out what is making them tick. You get an understanding of and feel for the community. You find out what turns people on and what irritates them. Through osmosis you absorb their experience, and it becomes *your* experience.

As I said, I learned something else, too. These men regarded insurance as a necessary evil. They had little respect for it, and even less for insurance agents. The reason became clear soon enough. Whenever agents called it was with one purpose in mind: to make a sale. If they succeeded, that was the end of it. It was the last the client would see of the agent for years. Once the policy was sold the agent was no longer interested. No one called on the businessman regularly.

These wealthy and successful entrepreneurs admitted to me time and again they had no real understanding of insurance. It hadn't been explained to them by their attorneys, accountants, or bankers. The agent who sold them a policy never discussed it in depth. The impression they got was that he knew no more about it than they did.

Slowly, gradually, it was beginning to crystalize. I could see it and feel it!

A tremendous void existed, a void that no one was filling.

The 25 agents in town were calling on the young, struggling wage earners. But no one was giving honest, concerned, professional attention to the successful and wealthy businessman who needed it most. Well, they were going to get that attention, I decided. They would get it from me.

The Transition from Package Salesman to Businessman

I decided something else, too. If you intend to do business with businessmen you ought to feel, act, and look the part of a businessman yourself.

I had been doing a lot of reading and studying. I had learned that a good businessman sets goals for himself. The goals I set were ambitious in the light of what I had accomplished to date. I decided I would write $500,000 during my first calendar year 1960, $750,000 the following year, and in the third year I would break one million.

In the months ahead I worked day and night to make each part of the structure I was designing solid, lasting, and strong. I spent six days a week calling on people, introducing myself, getting to know them and, hopefully, getting them to know me. I want to make it clear I didn't look on myself as a life insurance "salesman." I was attempting to build a reputation for myself as a person you could trust, like, and believe in. I worked at this task conscientiously long hours each week.

On top of that I officiated at basketball games during the season. I enjoyed this work and it was good for me, too. A lot of people saw me and came to know me by name. What's more, I was earning $15 to $18 a game, and that was much needed income.

At night when I got home from my calls or from working a game, I'd sit down and continue my studies, often into the early hours of the morning. Gradually I began to feel I was acquiring the depth of knowledge I would need to give service to people in business.

As the weeks and months passed I made another decision. For two and a half years I had my office at home. I had no secretary. I did all the paper work myself, the bookkeeping and correspondence.

One day I resolved to move into my own office downtown. A new professional building, the only one in town, had just been put up by two doctors. It was very important to me to be in that building. At first it looked as if there wouldn't be room for me. But I noticed on the floor plan that there was a 9 x 18-foot storage room at the back of the building, that was slated to be used for janitorial service and supplies. I talked the doctors into renting that space for $35 a month. They put up a little partition for me in the middle of it, which made two rooms, 9' x 8½'.

I had been growing increasingly embarrassed working out of my home. It was neither permanent nor professional. So this was a big step for me. I was proud of the new address on my stationery and calling cards. I was beginning to feel like a businessman.

I hired a secretary to come in a couple of hours a day to do typing and answer the telephone. A year later I was in a position to move into larger offices and hire a full-time secretary. But for the time being this was a major stride towards my ultimate goal.

Throughout those first three years my theories were constantly being put to the test. Other agents, package salesmen, some of them making fair livings, told me I was wasting my time, beating my brains out for nothing, that all my hard study and work would never pay off. There were many times when I doubted myself, wondered if what I was attempting made sense. I kept trying to widen the frame of the picture, but there were many who appeared determined to narrow it down.

Trial by Fire

Then all of a sudden it started to jell and any remaining self doubts dissolved. An important turning point in my life and career was the day when, following a lead in our local newspaper, I called on an optometrist in town. This gentleman, getting on in years, had taken in a junior partner. Next morning, newspaper announcement in hand, I visited his office and introduced myself. I congratulated him for taking on a partner and wished him luck. Then I said I would like to talk about it.

He thanked me and asked me what I meant. What did I want to talk about? Your buy-and-sell agreement, I replied. Oh, that. He said his attorney was handling it, couldn't see the point in talking to me. Well, I explained, not at all sure of the ground I was on, what I wanted to talk about was the insurance he would need for the buy-and-sell. He frowned. "What insurance do you mean?"

I knew very little myself, but what I knew I revealed. "Our company has insurance you and your partner own on each other. A provision in your buy-and-sell states that if something happens to either one of you, the money goes to the other partner and he can buy out the interest of the deceased."

"How much will it cost?"

I remembered the pledge I had made to myself about not telling people that I knew something when I didn't. I honestly said I didn't know.

All this time we were standing in the reception room. The doctor asked me to come back to his office. When I followed him down that long narrow hallway, it felt like the longest walk of my life because I didn't have the foggiest notion what I would say when we stopped walking.

We sat down and he asked me if I didn't have the rate information. I admitted I didn't, but said that if he could give me their birth dates and tell me how much the business was worth, I would get the information and bring it back the next day.

What I was buying was time. That afternoon I put a call in to Denver to find out what to do next. I had read enough about buy-and-sell agreements to understand the basics, but I felt what I knew was inadequate and the one thing I knew I didn't want to do was bluff. My general agent in Denver told me what to do step by step. Next day I went back and sat down with the partners. The policy came to $25,000 each on the two doctors, with over $2,000 of premium. They asked if medical examinations were necessary. They sure are, I replied. Very well. The optometrist buzzed his secretary and instructed her to make out the check for $2,000 plus.

I couldn't believe what had happened. It had all been so easy—no argument, no hassling through competitive bids and comparing with other agents' proposals. It was the easiest sale I had ever made—and the biggest.

In a very dramatic way it confirmed my feelings and basic assumptions about the business insurance market. This is the right way to do it, I said.

I never reversed this conclusion. For my first calendar year in the business I had targeted $500,000. I made it with $80,000 to spare. Shooting for $750,000 my second year, I actually wrote $800,000. For year number three I had set my goal at one million dollars worth of life insurance and membership in the Million Dollar Round Table. It was more than a wild dream of youth. That year I wrote $1,200,000 of qualified business.

Following my convictions and instincts, trying to provide a total professional service for every client I dealt with, trying to be something more than a salesman, I succeeded in placing myself among the elite of my industry. That year's MDRT meeting was held aboard the luxury ship "Kungsholm" sailing from New York to Bermuda. It was my first association with the giants of the industry, the legends I had been reading about throughout my three-year apprenticeship.

The trip turned out to be one of the great experiences of my life. I felt a heady pride in my accomplishments coupled with a challenging vision of how much remained to be done. I rubbed shoulders with people who were admired and respected nationwide. I stood eyeball to eyeball with professionals. My sights were raised and I was all but floating. Anything is possible, I thought. If you want it to happen, you can make it happen. There were times on that trip when I thought I had died and gone to heaven.

From that point on my career took off like a skyrocket. The following years totally confirmed and justified the method and premise I had worked so hard to develop. In my sixth year, still under 30, I wrote $7,000,000 and commanded the respect of the business community. In 1974, despite the fact that I spent seven months away from my headquarters in Sterling, I wrote over $20,000,000 of new business.

Can You Do It Too?

So what? Just because Lyle Blessman did it, that doesn't mean that you can do it too. Or does it?

It does IF—and the IF is a big one—IF your resolve is sufficiently strong, IF your philosophy and outlook are right.

You can make it to the Million Dollar Round Table and beyond. You can go on from there to double and quadruple the amount of business you write IF . . .

. . . IF, whatever the level at which you are presently operating, you are determined to climb.

. . . IF you are willing to work faithfully as I did and as I am still doing to develop the knowledge and expertise you will need to help people and win their respect.

. . . IF you are obsessed with a burning desire to

serve, to help others accomplish the goals they have set.

. . . IF, recognizing how much we all have to learn, you keep asking and probing and listening hard to the answers, trying the best you can to encourage people to define their problems and needs.

. . . IF, determined not to be walled in by trite and conventional boundaries, you expand your mind and become receptive to new ideas, approaches, and concepts.

. . . IF you stop waiting for that lucky break to occur and take action to *make it occur.* How? By realizing that the only way to get wet is to jump into the pool. In short, to get out there and *do it*!

I can tell you one thing about making it big in this industry or anywhere else. It is not done with mirrors. It is not done by conning people and by hard sell persuasion. I know of no magic solutions. It is done by first, *resolving* to do it, and next, by following through with the dedication and hard work that fuel the resolve with pure substance.

Can you do it IF these conditions are met? There is no doubt about it!

Here Is Why I'm So Sure

If anyone asked me the main reason I am writing this book I would have to say it's because I know for a fact that The Blessman Approach is transferable. I know that if I can do it, you can do it. All you need are the will and the staying power to prepare yourself properly. I know you can do it because I've watched others do it time and again, agents with average smarts and the right motivation.

Yes, there is one thing I do that most other agents don't do. I get inside the client's head. I find out who he is and what he needs. Then I direct all of my efforts to serve him.

If there is one thing I have learned it is this. It's not what you say that's important; it's *what you know and what you do*. It's what you say with your eyes and the way people read what you're saying. Your client can tell if you're comfortable with him and with yourself, if it's *you* that is speaking, or some contrived personality. Phoney. Insincere. He may never voice it or consciously acknowledge it even to himself. But he knows. It is something he senses.

If a business relationship isn't based on mutual trust, it isn't worth having. And if there is one thing The Blessman Approach will achieve, it is to make the agent believable.

As I said, I have lived through all of the hardships, worries, and fears any insurance agent could have experienced. I have been through the mill, and if I am anything at all, I'm a realist. I'm not speaking about "magic keys to success" from a pedestal. I have no psychic powers. I do not walk on water. I didn't make Princeton or Harvard and I'm no smarter than you are. I started out in this industry with no special training or skills.

My background and education as a physical education instructor gives me no special edge when it comes to selling insurance. However, I owe full credit to the NMC training program that spanned my first five years. My General Agent and Home Office staff alike were my sources of knowledge and confidence. I'm just an ordinary guy who learned the hard way what it takes to succeed in this business, and what I learned is transferable. I know it's transferable because I've repeatedly seen it transferred and in a little while I hope to prove it.

The point I'm trying to make is simply this. Anyone with a reasonable degree of intelligence who works and studies hard to gain the business, insurance, tax, and financial knowledge that's necessary, and refuses to settle for the status quo, can do the same thing that I did and more. That's all there is to it.

Is There an Ideal Location?

Is Sterling, Colorado and the area surrounding it the perfect place for an insurance agent to cover? Did I just by some kind of rare good fortune happen on this spot? Well, I was lucky indeed to have found Sterling because there's no place on earth I would rather call home. The people who live and work here are the kind of people I love, the kind who have made America great.

But when it comes to their needs relating to business financing, family obligations, and taxes, their problems are by no means unique. The people of Sterling have the same problems you will find in every state of this union, in big cities as well as small towns. Sterling is a cross-section of America. What I found here you'll find anywhere. What I was able to accomplish here, you can do in Bangor, Maine; Tuscaloosa, Alabama; New York City or Seattle.

Estate studies bear this out eloquently. It's not something I dreamed up; it's a matter of record. Studies published by the Estate Research Institute show that of 12,000 estates probated throughout the United States in 1977, three out of four had inadequate funding. Seventy-five percent. A quite substantial majority. That means that in three out of four cases families ran into hardship and considerable loss because, despite the deceased's considerable assets, they lacked the cash that was required to close out the estate.

Now you don't have to be very glib or persuasive to convince a businessman of the wisdom of preparing for this in advance instead of saddling his family with the headache at the worst possible time, the time of his death. You don't even have to sell him. It is plain common sense. All he needs are the facts. But as I said, what most often happens is that the businessman himself is usually too hectically involved in his business to dig out the facts. And even if this isn't the case, he's only vaguely aware of the problem if he has any awareness at all. The truth of the matter is that neither his lawyer, accountant, banker, or insurance agent if he has one, takes the time to discuss it with him. So it remains neglected year after year.

This places you, as the knowledgeable insurance agent with an honest desire to serve your client, in a uniquely favorable position.

There is clearly a job to be done and a priceless service to be rendered to millions of businessmen all over America. I discovered this my first year in the business and it is as true today as it was then. A void exists that is fairly begging to be filled. It presents an unprecedented challenge to life underwriters and the kind of opportunity that can make one's head reel. Seventy-five percent of all successful and affluent businessmen are being ignored or neglected. There's enough work for everyone.

The Live Evidence

Is the so-called Blessman Approach universally applicable? In the end this is the critical question. If you don't apply it, you're wasting your time reading this book. If you can apply it, it may change your whole life. But how can you be sure adopting the concept and following the methods I recommend doesn't require some unique talent or super-high level of intelligence to comprehend what I'm doing and do the same thing yourself? If you want proof that what I preach is transferable, and I think getting proof is important, I can think of no more convincing evidence than to cite live examples of agents who are using it successfully. It is a very small sample chosen at random. I hope the experience, comments, and thoughts of these men will be helpful.

Example No. 1

THE AGENT — Ed Frantz, Wichita, Kansas

BACKGROUND AND COMMENTS: Ed is a Northwestern Mutual agent. My close association with him dates back to about 1967. At the time he was convinced he could never write more than a million or a million-and-a-half dollars worth of business a year. We had several long discussions about our respective methods and philosophies of doing business. At the outset Ed was quite negative about my ideas being transferable.

Ed Frantz: "You work in a specialized agricultural market; I work in an urban area in Wichita. You know all those people in Sterling. It isn't easy for me to walk into somebody's office and start to make conversation."

I insisted my ideas were transferable wherever you worked. I kept encouraging him: "You can do it, Ed. I know you can. You may have to do it a little differently than I do it. But you can use the ideas."

After many conversations, Ed started to try my ideas. "They had a real influence on me," he told an associate of mine recently. "I mean a real impact. Today

I'm convinced his ideas are transferable. He talked an awful lot about stretching your mind, and that is one concept I definitely learned from Lyle. I used to tell myself I could never do more than a million or two, and he convinced me I could do more if I believed I could do it. I used a lot of Lyle's ideas, and I'm still using them today.

"Over the years, I was able to see that there are a lot of people out here in Wichita or wherever you are who have large problems. They are basically liquidity problems. When a man dies he owes the government a lot of money, and often his estate doesn't have the liquidity to pay it. Or the liquidity is lacking to fund a buy-sell agreement in a closely held corporation. In most situations—95 percent of the time—life insurance is the logical answer. There are an awful lot of people out there with a great deal of problems.

"Another thing I learned from Lyle is the importance of listening. If we are good listeners people will tell us more in many cases than they will tell their other financial advisers. If we will just be quiet and listen, we will learn what people want to do to solve their problems, to take care of their wives and children and their estates. If we come up with the right solution they will buy. It's not actually selling. People don't really buy life insurance; in many cases they literally take it from you."

As well as almost anyone I know, Ed has learned how to serve clients over the years and to serve them continuously. "As a result," he says, "I have grown with them, both in terms of knowledge and education and the business I do. It's what I call a natural evolution."

RESULT: Ed Frantz is now at the $7 million level and keeps climbing each year.

Example No. 2

THE AGENT: Jim Altenbern, Fort Morgan, Colo.

BACKGROUND AND COMMENTS: Jim was born and raised in Chicago. At 44 years of age he already had been employed by four different insurance companies. The son of a successful businessman, he was accustomed to luxurious living, a great conversationalist, an outstanding golfer. Yet despite a fine formal education, good personality, and tremendous talent, he was basically lacking in confidence, not at ease with his clients. He lacked the patience to probe problems in depth. He constantly pushed for the sale, the "close," the name on the dotted line. A chain smoker, he had to sit on his hands. He also worked for The Northwestern. When I was out his way at times we would talk. Jim was itching and restless, a keg of dynamite. I was cool, looking half asleep by comparison.

We did a few cases together, Jim finding it hard to sit still. How much longer will it take? When are you going to sell him? He almost went out of his mind. This approach is by no means unique. I've seen it time and again. Instead of probing the client's need, the average agent will have only one thought in mind: his own need, the wife and five kids to support, the need to chalk up that sale, to earn that commission. The Blessman Approach doesn't work that way, I told Jim. The sale comes. But you don't force it. It comes naturally.

I think I helped to show Jim the importance of patience, a foundation block of the system I preach. The last case we did together, we wrote $108,000 on two lives. It took six months to set up the policy. I took Jim with me every time I went in because the case was in his area and I needed some help. Some of my ideas rubbed off on Jim, and he is using them today to expand both his mind and his business.

RESULT: Jim Altenbern is now writing upwards of $3 million a year.

Example No. 3

THE AGENT: John Spence, Sterling, Colorado

BACKGROUND AND COMMENTS: John and I have a great deal in common. We both started in teaching. We both have a desire and need to help people. John's first teaching job paid him $319 a month, $105 of which went for the rent. After his first child was born, he knew what it was to be up against it financially. He eventually took a job in the Social Sciences Department of the junior college in Sterling. As much as he liked teaching, one day he took a hard look at a bunch of guys ten years older than he who weren't doing much better financially. He decided it was time for a change.

In 1973 he started exploring other opportunities. One day he read an article in the local paper about what I was doing and how I used to be a teacher. He figured it might be a good idea to talk to me and get my advice. He came down and explained his situation and I gave him some life insurance material to read. To make a long story short, I wound up hiring him.

During the weeks that followed he learned how I worked, the importance of going all the way with a client, building a complete program, coordinating it with the client's attorney and financial people, and all the rest. John was a natural right from the start because his desire was not to peddle policies but to be of service. And even though there are basic differences in the way we do business, he was able to take the main elements of my approach and tailor them to his own personality and style.

I have always found John a great guy to converse

with. Well, one day with this book in mind, we hooked up a tape recorder to get some of his thoughts on a cassette.

John Spence: "I once got involved for a very short period of time with an outfit that sold vacuum cleaners with a canned sales presentation. After that I decided I couldn't sell anything. After observing the methods of those other agents, I repeatedly thank the good Lord that we work the way we do."

"You know, one of the things you develop is a sensitivity to what people want. You have to get to the point where the client feels comfortable. I find that the more you talk with a man about his needs, and the more he asks you what you think ought to be done, the more of his confidence you win. You begin to feel you can give some direction. None of this is ever done with the traditional cold canvass, hit him over the head, grab his attention approach."

"When people ask me if I miss teaching I tell them I'm not really doing anything that different now, except that I'm teaching insurance to people who benefit a great deal from the knowledge."

"Last week I sold about $135,000 worth of life insurance .... My salary almost doubled in the past two years. It does a good deal for your self-image. I feel a lot better about myself than I did a couple of years ago. You can extend the professional approach into wider and wider circles, serving more and more people, basically without any prospecting. You know, the woods are full of people out there. You don't have to beat your brains out to get to them."

"Not only does it provide for my family, but I know I'm helping the people who need help. And there's the thrill and excitement of the financial thing, being able to see beyond the dollars and cents. It gets to you after a while—the client's confidence."

John adds his own special touches and unique individuality to the way he deals with people. But basicaly, when you distill it right down to his essence, in his own modified manner he is applying The Blessman Approach.

RESULT: John is now doing close to $2 million a year, and he is still relatively new in the business.

Example No. 4

THE AGENT: Roy Williams, Stockton, California

BACKGROUND AND COMMENTS: Roy, who has several people working for him, and a lawyer on his staff, runs his operation much the way I run mine. A former gridiron star, he is six foot seven inches tall and weighs 280 pounds. He is strongly opposed to the time worn high pressure, quick sale, peddler approach. Like me, he is devoting a great deal of time and effort to upgrade the image and professionalism of the insurance industry. Some of the comments he expressed when he learned I was writing this book help, I think, to provide insights into the way this professional approach I keep talking about works and the values it brings.

Roy Williams: "After rapping with Lyle at AALU and MDRT meetings I was able to use some of his ideas in working with people . . . . He comes in and sits down as quickly as possible so he doesn't physically intimidate them. He does things very simply, works easily with the lawyers and accountants. He doesn't try to overwhelm them. Attorneys get their backs up when you drag out information. You can't suggest that you know more than they know. You have to be able to guide the questions. The way Lyle does this, they don't get embarrassed in front of their clients. He makes the lawyer and accountant look like heroes. And he does it without trying to manipulate them."

Traditionally, Roy said, the insurance industry goes by the numbers. "You see a hundred people a day, you're going to sell two. Now that to me is asinine. You don't sell anything, you solve people's problems. If you solve their problems, they're going to buy. So I think the trend is changing. The industry has to change.

"The one thing that the insurance industry has, that I have not seen in any other business, is the open sharing—between companies, between agents. Nobody holds anything back. Everything I've ever asked Lyle for he's given me. It's just incredible.

"Lyle listens. I'd say that is one of his best attributes.

"We're in a little town and people say that makes you different. It makes no difference at all. I feel I could go anywhere in the country and in 60 days be doing what I'm doing here. I could go to Los Angeles or San Francisco and do the same thing.

"It's appalling, isn't it? The rich and super rich in this country are getting no advice. None. The lawyers are too busy putting out fires for their clients. Accountants are too busy doing accounting and tax work. Nobody's advising their clients in estate and business planning, and I don't care whether you're talking about New York and Detroit or Stockton, California and Sterling. The problem is almost identical.

"People are starving for professional help. If you want to help people, they're available."

RESULT: Following these precepts and beliefs, Roy

Williams is one of the most successful life insurance agents in this country. As is the case with my own operation, most of his business comes from existing clients whom he continues to serve using the coordinated total services approach.

Is It Time for a Change?

Charles Kettering once said, "The world hates change, yet it is the only thing that has brought progress."

It's what brought progress to me.

If you are among the thousands of agents who up to now have been peddling policies instead of helping people, you have a decision to make that could affect your whole life. Do you want to continue peddling policies? If so, that's up to you. But if you want to serve others, and serve yourself in the process, you will first have to change your attitude and approach.

I never said it would be easy, and I never said it could be done overnight. It will require hard work, determination, and time. It's a matter of planning and building, slowly, patiently, a step at a time. It's a matter of solving problems and filling needs. It's a matter of serving, not selling. Serve sincerely and faithfully and the sales will take care of themselves.

Is it time for a change?

It's your decision to make. And it's for you to decide if it's worth the dedication and effort. It's for you to decide if the job you hold now is a stop gap until that lucky break comes along, or a step in your career journey upward. I know what the decision entails because I made it myself. And I never regretted it. And I never regretted or apologized for being a part of this industry. I can hold my head high because I know I help people. And I know another thing too.

Helping people helps me most of all.

3.

WHO I WAS —
WHO I AM

You may have wondered as you picked up this book: Who is this guy, Lyle Blessman? What qualifies him to write a book telling others how to do business and how not to do business? What are his credentials?

A logical and reasonable question. In recent years, as a life underwriter, I have been writing business in the neighborhood of $18-$20 million a year. That may sound impressive. But does it qualify me as an expert, or give me the authority to write a book?

Not necessarily.

Only one question is of relevance to you: "Can I do what he did?"

I firmly believe that you can if your desire is strong enough and your willingness to work hard and make sacrifices great enough. I don't have to tell you that in the insurance profession as in others, when a person is very successful, a mystique often builds up around him. The illusion develops that he is separate and apart from the rest of the world. Twenty million, people think, wow! The guy must have been the recipient of some remarkable kind of good luck. Or he's eight feet tall, has two heads, graduated summa cum laude from Harvard, and walks on water for exercise. That's simply not true of most super pros that I know. It's certainly not true of me.

If anything at all qualifies me to write this book, it is not the fact that I write $20 million worth of business a year. That is simply a byproduct of The Blessman Approach. What qualifies me most of all, I believe, is that I have been through the mill. I have known anxiety, fear, and despair in their most insidious forms. Whatever you may have gone through as an agent, whatever you may be going through now, I can understand you and empathize, for I have been there myself. Since the early days of my childhood and as far back as I can remember, I have lived with hardship and strife. I have bled with the best of them. This, I think, is my most important credential.

The Early Days

I am a Coloradian by transplant. I was born April 29, 1936 in central Illinois about 165 miles south of Chicago. The closest city of any size was Lincoln. This is agricultural country and my dad was a tenant farmer. Talk about poor. I think we invented the word. We lived in houses they would burn down today. I was the youngest of three boys. Although my dad always farmed, he never owned his own place. He was always the hired man. The most he ever earned in his life was $300 a month. He lived in poverty and died broke. The most important thing in his life, he always said, more important than money, was to have people think well of him.

This wasn't always easy to come by. I have no intention in this book or elsewhere to reveal the sordid details of my childhood or to make a big pitch for sympathy. It is enough to say that my father was a mean, hard drinking man, embittered by his losing battle with life.

My main ambition from the time I was ten or eleven was to somehow escape from that meanness, hardship, and poverty. I was afraid of life and even more fearful of people. But the idea of running away became a compulsion. I had to get away from my father's lifestyle and crawl out of that trap. My mother had a great influence on my optimism and gave me mental support and hope whenever she could within her means.

Yet no one I have ever met is all bad or all good. My dad had his compensating virtues. He taught me two things (unknowingly, I believe) for which I am grateful.

Today in retrospect I can say that the ability to apply oneself to the hard unpleasant tasks of life, the tasks no one else wants to do, is one of the prime keys to success. I had to learn this the hard way, but the important thing is I learned it and sometimes I think the hard way is the best way of all. My father taught me to work and not leave the job until it was done. I learned to tackle any task I was given, however tough and unpleasant, because it was the only option I had. The consequences of refusing the job were too fearful to contemplate.

Another thing I learned from my dad was integrity. The cardinal sin in his eyes was to lie or take something you didn't earn or was not rightfully yours. I can thank him for that.

Searching Hard for the Sunshine

I consider myself very lucky. Hard times are the world's greatest teacher. If, as has been said, adversity introduces a man to himself, I must have met myself head on.

Adversity will make one person bitter and cynical, a malevolent hater, the next person more resolute. I became intensely determined. Deep down inside of me I knew there was a better world to be found. I didn't know where it was or how I would reach it, but somehow I would get there. I lived for the day I could walk into the sunshine. Instead of scarring me as they well might have done, the childhood conditions I was forced to endure helped to shape and mold me, and added a kind of purpose to my life.

When I was in grade school (which was a one-room country school), the farm my dad worked at was next to a golf course. Every chance I could get I would go over there and caddy for the doctors and businessmen who belonged to the club. They would drive up in their big new cars, wearing finer clothes than I had ever seen in my life. They would always have money for drinks and for a bottle of soda pop for the caddy.

I would listen greedily as they discussed the things they had done with their families, the holidays and vacations they planned, the shows they had seen or were going to see, the University of Illinois game they would attend the following Saturday. And I would think, there *is* more to life. People *can* be friendly, decent, kind, and full of *love*.

I kept listening and observing their actions. I would

try to imitate their manners and speech. It was a habit I formed early in life. When I didn't know what was proper and acceptable, I would listen and watch and take the cue from what I observed. I noticed that these people at the golf club didn't interrupt while another person was speaking. They were rarely profane and vulgar. Men opened doors for the ladies. It was a new world for me. These people were well dressed and well mannered. I felt the way they were acting must be the right way to act. So I tried to act the same way.

Every once in a while one of the doctors or businessmen I caddied for would go off to a tournament at some other club, for the day, or perhaps for the weekend. And he would take me with him to caddy. Think of that. All I did was carry his bag. But he thought enough of me to take me with him. That was really something to me. It gave me something to think about.

I began attending Sunday church services at the First Christian Church in town three or four miles down the road from the farm. I didn't have to go; my family didn't even belong to the church as my father wouldn't let my mother attend. I went because I wanted to go, because some of the people I caddied for belonged to that church. I would watch the people and imitate the way that they acted. It made me feel good. Each Sunday during the singing of the hymn non-members would get up and walk down to the front of the church if they wanted to join the church and be baptized. The third or fourth time I was there I got up and walked to the front of the church and asked to join and to be baptized.

At that age, 12 or 13, I didn't know about God or religion. But darn it, those people seemed happy. They seemed decent and clean. There was no hollering there, no beatings, no meanness, at least none that I could see. They didn't know where I came from and they didn't ask. I wanted very much to be like them. I wanted them to accept me and approve of me. And they did.

Since my early childhood, I suppose, I always searched hard for the sunshine. It was a search I never abandoned and perhaps my persistence was another trait I learned from my dad. Whatever else he may have been, he was never a quitter of the job at hand. He hung in there tenaciously, and whenever there was something I knew I wanted in life, I learned to do the same thing.

Needless to say, in those days my goals weren't clearly defined. Unconsciously, gropingly, I worked and struggled in an effort to climb out of that trap. As a freshman in high school I did odd jobs any time I could find them, washing milk bottles at a dairy, caddying, picking corn by hand, scooping corn on a corn sheller. No job was too low or too menial. Any money I got was money I earned for myself. And I took pride in my appearance, in the impression I made on others. I wanted to be somebody. I wanted people to think well of me.

High school introduced me to athletics. I felt the urge to compete. In high school I played football and basketball and went out for track. Here, too, the hard work and persistence paid off. I never missed a competition or game and won letters in all three sports. I was elected team captain two years on my football team. We shared the basketball conference title my senior year.

College and Connie

Because of my athletic record and size (I'm six foot six inches tall), I had the opportunity to go to college on a scholarship. No one on either side of my family had ever been to college or even considered it because of how much it would cost. But I began getting scholarship offers from colleges that wanted me to play football or basketball. After visiting a number of campuses I wound up at DePauw University in Greencastle, Indiana, on a full basketball scholarship.

After one year at DePauw, the basketball coach at Colorado State University contacted me through an alumnus and invited me to come out to Colorado even though I would have to sit out for a year before being eligible to play. Well, there I was, a farm kid from central Illinois who hadn't been 50 miles from home before going off to DePauw now going to Colorado State, a bigger school with a basketball team that played in a tougher conference. The idea of going to a big important school such a long way from home was heady fare indeed.

I packed my three bags at the end of my freshman year at DePauw and headed west of the Mississippi for the first time in my life. There I found an entire new world and experienced things I hadn't even dared dream about. I played basketball there for two years and earned my college letter jacket. But off campus I was never too proud to work, so I washed dishes and collected garbage at the student union to pay for my clothes and the living expenses that weren't covered by the scholarship.

The best thing that happened to me at Colorado State was meeting Connie, my future wife. We were married in June, right after graduation. In the fall we went down to Durango, Colorado to embark on the career I had enthusiastically decided to follow, that of a basketball coach and biology teacher. I had a great deal of ambition and was loaded with idealism. I had decided that I was going to be an outstanding teacher and a great basketball coach. But I'm sure you know what has been said about "the best laid plans of mice and men."

After a few months passed by I faced the realization that however rewarding teaching and coaching might be from a psychological standpoint, the prospects of making a decent living would be bleak for many years to come. That's when, as I mentioned earlier, after contacting the old gentleman from Northwestern Mutual Life Insurance Co. who had been of so much help to Connie's mother in her time of great need, I decided it might be a good idea to go into the life insurance business. It looked particularly appealing to me at the time because I was given to understand it would require no capital to get started.

As it turned out, a new general agent had just been appointed in Denver, and I got in touch with him. He sent me a series of aptitude tests which I completed and returned through the mail. I never found out if I scored well or, as a new general agent, he was on the lookout for warm bodies. Whatever the case, I was accepted. We loaded our meager belongings into worn valises and cartons and, with a three-month-old daughter, headed out for Sterling.

The Emerging Philosophy

I came to Sterling as a virtual stranger at the age of 23 on June 23, 1959. The only person I knew there was my mother-in-law. My knowledge of the life insurance business at the time could have been written on the back of a matchbook cover. I had no previous experience, no office to work from, and only a college notebook containing my applications, medicals, and insured savings proposals to use as a briefcase.

But I fell in love with Sterling from the start. Raised as an Illinois farm boy, it was the kind of community I was accustomed to. The people there were my kind of people.

I just started walking and driving up and down the

roadways and streets, introducing myself to everyone I ran into, getting acquainted, talking about everything except life insurance, a subject I didn't know too much about.

The first six months I went strictly by the book, the traditionalist, making the package selling pitch I had learned by rote in my quick training program. I made 857 calls, some night, some day, as I mentioned earlier, during those six months, and 25 sales for an unimpressive total volume of $174,000. Not a promising start. During one seven-week period, as I said, I made only two sales. One was a $5,000 policy, the other a $10,000 policy. The $10,000 application was declined. Around that time my business—and me along with it—came pretty close to falling apart.

Results or not, however, I worked at it very religiously. And call reluctance or not, I was somehow or other always in contact with people. Most of the people I called on were at day jobs during the week. I worked four nights a week. That left three nights. Two of those nights during the basketball season I officiated at games. I loved doing it and I thought it was good for me to do, because I got to know a lot of people and they got to know me, who I was, what it was I did for a living.

Equally important I earned $15 to $18 per game and that extra $30 or $40 in weekly income was desperately needed at the time with a new baby at home. During those early years I would work like thunder and, after getting in at 9:00, 10:00, or 11:00 from my calls or a game, I would read and try to learn the business I was in.

How long did it take for my philosophy—the so-called Blessman Approach—to develop and jell? I would say about three years or so. During this time I kept plodding along, making adjustments, cracking those books, and arriving at certain conclusions that challenged the traditional concepts, the package selling approach. The "experts" kept telling me I was crazy. They wrote up their fives and tens, trundling along in the conventional way without knocking themselves out. My system, they said, which opposed the hit-and-run hard sell approach, just wouldn't work.

Well, it seems to have worked all right, if $20 million dollars worth of business in a single year and a long list of loyal clients who have stuck with me over the years are any indication of success. It worked for me, and it can work for you too.

Well, what is it we're talking about? What is The Blessman Approach? What does the philosophy add up to? The following chapters of this book will outline the techniques and procedures on a step by step basis. But the mechanics of any approach are meaningless unless they are built on a strong and sturdy foundation. The foundation for The Blessman Approach is capsulized in the following simple precepts and guidelines. Here in a nutshell, before we get into the actual nuts and bolts of the system, is what my philosophy of business in general and selling life insurance in particular is all about. And you might say it sums up my approach to living as well.

The Ten Guidelines I Work and Live By

1. Deal with people you care deeply about.
2. Dare to be different.
3. Never stop being a student.
4. Find the client who needs you.
5. Spread sunshine wherever you go.
6. Absorb experience like a sponge.

7. Keep your foot out of the door.

8. Adopt the I-sure-as-hell-can-do-it mentality.

9. Face up to your weaknesses.

10. Face the hard realities of business life.

Deal With the People You Care Deeply About

This guideline is at the top of my list for a very good reason. I can think of no credo more important or meaningful.

I hope it will not be construed as snobbishness when I say that I am very selective in deciding with whom I will do business and whose business I will refuse to pursue. I don't care how wealthy a person may be. If we're not compatible, if he doesn't like me and I don't care for him, our relationship cannot be successful. If he is arrogant, or feels I'm beneath him, or expects me to be beholden to him for the business he favors me with, even if I could sell him a $2 million policy, I wouldn't be interested.

I don't want the client who would let me know that if it weren't for his business I wouldn't be able to fly around in the airplane I own. If the relationship isn't genuinely and honestly enthusiastic on both sides, I don't need it or want it. I firmly believe that if you took away all my financial and material assets, but left me the friends I have made and the confidence they have developed in me, I would have no problem rebuilding. If you deprived me of my friends and left me all of my money and things, I would be bankrupt.

In both business and life my primary, overriding concern centers on the people I deal with, and work with, and know. I am a bit fanatical, I suppose, on this subject of friendship. A friend, in proving his friendship, should bear his friend's problems and woes. When I think of a friend, I think of him not for a day or a week but for a lifetime. From my earliest days as an agent I was turned off by the hit-and-run salesman, the agent who gets the client's name on a contract and then forgets about him. If you care about people, you stick with them through good and bad. Adhering to this precept is the only way I could ever do business.

If I count a man as my friend I want to know how he's feeling and thinking. It's been said that friendship is tried in need. Trying to anticipate the needs of my friends and clients, I make it my business to keep in touch on a regular basis. For about five years I had a two-way radio hookup in my car, tied into my office and home. I was always in contact, wherever I was. After hours Connie would intercept the calls. Only after I started spending a great deal of time in the office did I discontinue the system.

It satisfies a personal need that I have to get vibes from my clients that tell me everything is all right. If I don't get the vibes, if my instinct tells me a friend may be upset or in trouble, I can't rest until I stop by to find out what's wrong.

When you genuinely and honestly care, a friend reads you and knows that you care. When he knows, he responds, and you know that he cares as well, and in the final reckoning that's what it's all about.

Dare To Be Different

America, I am convinced, is still the land of golden opportunity, however corny that may sound to some people. And if there is one occupation where I know this contention applies, it is the insurance profession. But to cash in on the promise, you have to strike the right approach for you and develop a modus operandi you can live with.

The typical hit-and-run agent has been trained to take his rate book, application, and documents, and zero in on a limited market in a limited way. He never learned to see the whole picture.

I was no different, believe me. During the early months of my career I fell into the same mindless routine because I had been preconditioned accordingly, and because it was the "path of least resistance," requiring a minimum of imagination and original thought. And I reaped the woes and hardships this path so often produces. It was only when I found the courage to be my own man and to do something different that success started coming my way.

It took no special perspicacity to reach the conclusion that the packaged approach wasn't working and wasn't going to work for me. This left three options open to me: 1) I could continue with the status quo and be a marginal performer all my life. 2) I could quit the profession altogether and seek another kind of work. 3) I could find a different way, a better way, to function effectively as a life insurance agent.

The status quo made no sense to me; it had no appeal and no future. Quitting simply wasn't part of my nature. Thus the third option was the only choice left. It started with exploring and assessing the market and eventually evolved into the total coordinated financial planning and management system described in this book. It involved changing my work habits and the age group I served, took me into the business insurance and estate planning aspects of the industry. Under this revised approach I would deal with clients who had the financial wherewithal to fulfill the needs that they had. I would remain with these clients throughout all of their lives as both advisor and friend. And if my approach worked the way I hoped it would, it would put a virtual end to cold canvas calls and permit me to work on leads referred by people who knew and had confidence in me.

The traditional process of selling life insurance—the numbers game that relied on the averages, the packaged selling pitches, the pressure cooker foot-in-the-door techniques—long had disturbed me. I had gone through that process, it's what I found when I entered the business, and I found it wanting, confining, and limiting.

The move into this new market of older business and professional people would require an immense amount of study, dedication, and hard work. But I had faith in its outcome and figured it would be well worth the effort.

Never Stop Being a Student

One of the most important things I did that was different, that I saw very few agents doing, was to study religiously, sometimes until one or two in the morning. No matter how busy I was, I always managed to find the time to be a student. And the most interesting thing I discovered very early in my career was that the learning process in business is altogether different from the learning process in college. There you take course after course year after year, and you go on accumulating credits until you have enough of them to graduate. But here I was reading and studying the intricacies of partnership insurance, key man insurance, corporation insurance, and insurance designed to provide estate liquidity, and what I learned about a problem and its solution at night I was able to apply the next day.

I took all the Northwestern courses I could. I read whatever I could lay my hands on about the advanced underwriting uses of life insurance. Then I put what I had learned into practice. I didn't score every time. I had my disappointments just as every agent does. But I kept plugging away, trying to get to the root of peoples' problems, asking questions and cracking books to come up with solutions. And when I hit on a solution to a businessman's problem which I did more and more frequently, I can tell you it was the most wonderful feeling in the world. I began to feel I was making a real contribution. I was educating people, telling them what they needed to know, instead of trying to scare them into accepting a product they couldn't afford.

When I first started I knew very little about business or tax planning. During my first six months I had been primarily concerned with basic training and just learning the ropes. In reading about the big names in the industry, I kept running across the phrase, "business insurance." I didn't know what it was and asked my general agent about it and how insurance was used in tax planning. He laughed and told me to forget about it. The subject was too advanced for a novice. There were courses on that, but they weren't scheduled to come for another three years.

"Hey, John," I told him. "Come on! I can't wait three years. I want those courses today."

So I talked him into sending me instructional literature on partnership insurance and insurance for corporations. That's how I began learning about business financing and liquidity and how life insurance ties into it. I kept studying as hard as I could to become as knowledgeable as possible in the shortest period of time. And I can tell you from experience that truly serving the client entails a never-ending quest for knowledge even in the basic areas; with tax reform it is compounded. I study more today than I ever did before, and with the knowledge explosion and the changing tax and business rules, I find that no matter how much you study you are always behind.

Another way I picked up valuable knowledge was by talking with people. The first thing I let them know was that I hadn't called on them to sell them insurance. I wanted to know what had made them successful, what observations and insights they could pass on to me about the business community. As a new agent you can do this anywhere and you will always learn and benefit from it. You can walk up to a mature, successful businessman and say, "I'm trying to get started in the life insurance business and I need someone wiser and more experienced than myself to talk to, someone who will give me advice."

A business or professional man is usually flattered by this frank and humble approach. And if you are young as I was then, he will probably be happy to adopt the role of advisor and father. In any case, in this way I learned all kinds of things about how to do business, about banking and financing and customer relations. They told me what was important to them and what was unimportant. They revealed the mistakes they had made as young men, and mistakes they had seen others make. And above all, I learned, was the sanctity of keeping your word, and it was something I never forgot.

Find the Client Who Needs You

All right, I have said this before and I will say it again. If I say it ten thousand times it will not be too often.

Find the Client Who Needs You!

Let us make some assumptions. You're a conscientious, hard working guy. You're a student, a learner, you sop up knowledge like a sponge. You like people and people like you. You're decent and ethical, a man whose word is his bond, and your image is important to you. On top of that you're articulate and persuasive. Anyone reading your profile would conclude you have a great deal going for you as an agent and salesman.

Still you are not making out, or you are not reaching the potential you feel that you should. Why not?

The odds are high that you have not found your right market. You are calling on people who either do not need your product or, if they do need it, can't afford the price that it costs.

I had to learn this the hard way and it's one of the most important conclusions I ever reached. You can't sell snow shoes on a tropical island. I already mentioned that when I came to Sterling I found 25 insurance companies serving that relatively small area and 25 agents pounding the pavement. This might well have been one of the most highly concentrated insurance markets in the country. Well, on the one hand, I concluded, there's not enough business to go around. On the other, most of the people those 25 agents are calling on couldn't afford the product even if they knew that they needed it. Insurance ranks very low on their list of priorities.

Yet the 25 agents kept hammering away with their hit-and-run foot-in-the-door approach. And I don't care who you set up as an example, you can take the most talented, knowledgeable, persuasive insurance agent in the world, if the market isn't there, he may do a little better than his competitors. But he will never reach his potential. It's like milking blood from a stone.

Spread Sunshine Wherever You Go

The novelist and playwright Henry Miller once said, "There is power in a smile. Smile and you are immediately happy. It is one of the best relaxation exercises I know."

Over 19 centuries ago the Roman poet, Ovid, wrote that burdens become light when they are cheerfully borne. And the historian and philosopher Carlyle referred to cheerfulness as the greatest of everyday virtues.

Good cheer is contagious, it adds to the happiness of others. An optimistic attitude is a reflection of good health; when you grumble and gripe you invite all kinds of trouble.

There's a story I am quite fond of telling. After I became succesful and established in Sterling, a Culligan dealer used to drive by my office each morning. He was a young man like myself who had started out three or four years after I did and we became good friends. We sometimes would go off on holidays together, and he was part of the closely knit group I played cards with each month.

Summer mornings I am usually out on the lawn that fronts the Blessman office building, and Gordon Jones would pass by at eight a.m. or so on his way to open the store. He would sometimes pull over to stop for a chat. As often as not he would ask, "How's business? How are things going?" And my invariable reply would be, "Great!," "Super!," something like that. I'm always enthusiastic and excited by nature; that's the kind of a guy I am. I smile and laugh a good deal.

Well, this little exchange went on for so long, it eventually got to old Gordon. One day he said, "For the love of Mike, Lyle, either you're some kind of phenomenon, or you're a darn good liar. You always have this smile on your face. You always look happy. Things can't *always* be great. You gotta have some bad days."

I answered, "Sure I have my bad days. Everyone does. There are days I don't feel well. There are days I have disappointments. But you're never going to know about it. You have your own problems, right? You don't have to hear about mine. Would it make you feel good to know that I have problems too?

He laughed, "I don't know. But sometimes I wish you would have just one bad day so I don't feel I'm the only one."

It's an interesting comment. Misery does enjoy company, I suppose, to a certain degree. But I think the fruits you get from good cheer are far more therapeutic. There's enough gloom and doom in this world. Poverty and racial unrest are still with us. Stories about corruption in high places seem to break every day. Creeping inflation persists. You can't turn the tube on before dinner without being exposed to accounts of murder and rape and man's inhumanity to man.

If I come out to see you, we're going to talk about your interests and affairs. You won't hear me saying, "Hey, Bill, I don't know how you can stay in business with interest up another two percent." If there's one thing you don't need it is someone reminding you how rotten things are and what lousy shape you are in. I once heard somebody say that a smile is a curve that can set a lot of things straight. That's the premise I go by.

Absorb Experience Like a Sponge

Experience to a salesman is like working capital is to an entrepreneur. Without it you can't grow and advance.

Education will help to advance your career. Reading and study will help. But the best teacher of all is experience. As Homer once wrote, after the event, even a fool is wise. Experience is the fertilizer that cultivates the lawn of your mind.

I know agents who feel cheated and limited because they lack a higher formal education. I won't pretend it's no handicap, but it is one that can be overcome by getting out there and doing the job. Education only prepares you for the career you select, but mostly you learn through osmosis, by seeing how other men operate and by following through on your own plans and ideas by doing things for yourself.

In my own case my college degree in physical education did very little to help my career as an agent except for the teaching and coaching skills. What molded me into a professional was getting into the midst of the action, talking to people and observing, learning something new from my studies one day and going out the next day to apply it.

Keep Your Foot Out of the Door

During the past ten years I have been speaking regularly from platforms all over the country at marketing seminars and sales conferences. One of my main motivations is the hope that I might play a small role in changing the longstanding negative image the salesman has in the eyes of many businessmen and the public, particularly young people starting out on careers on their own. In college, for example, when considering their futures, very few opt for selling. In the average mind the insurance agent or sales rep is associated with the Willie Loman type of "drummer" who uses high pressure tactics, gimmicks, hot selling phrases, and has a superficial get-the-order-at-all-costs personality. If not an out and out con man, he's at least a shade short of ethical.

It's an image that deeply disturbs me. I think it has improved somewhat in recent years. In insurance and some other industries, professionalism is being preached more and more from speakers' platforms, in magazine articles and books on salesmanship. And it has increasingly become a part of sales training programs. The CLU movement and the MDRT has done much to improve the image of the agent.

Yet the image continues to cling and will be a long time in dying.

I believe the foot-in-the-door salesman is on his way out in America. The public is wise to him. The buyer will no longer succumb to his tactics. Admittedly, a handful of pressure tacticians have been highly successful. Compelling because of their immense egos, unshakable purpose, single minded ambition and drive, they virtually mow down sales resistance by sheer force of their personality and will. At a sales conference recently at which I was scheduled to speak, the speaker before me, an egocentric old war horse, had stirred up the audience with his fiery message which advocated overwhelming prospects with techniques combining gimmickry, fear, and double talking persuasion and emotionalism.

My own talk, following his was quiet and reasoned in contrast. Its main theme was professionalism, the new selling approach based on helping and serving the client instead of beating him down to the ground. I was walking on eggshells in taking that posture after a speech filled with thunder and lightning. But I was saying what I thought had to be said and I let it pour out spontaneously, not sure how it would be received. How it *was* received is an indication of the times and the change taking place. I got a standing ovation.

It took me three years to design my philosophy, an approach that is free of empty gimmicks and showmanship. I worked day and night and weekends as well to refine it, making great sacrifices in the process. But what emerged is sound and effective. Most important, it has stood up well under time's acid test.

Adopt the I-Sure-As-Hell-Can-Do-It Mentality

You are as big as the picture you paint for yourself.

The world's great achievers in whatever field you could name are the men and women who set personal goals that in some measure exceed what they imagine their limits to be, who refuse to admit to themselves the possibility of failure.

I set for myself a goal of a half million dollars for my first calendar year, three-quarters of a million the second year, and one million the third year. In each case I exceeded my goal and have been setting and exceeding goals ever since.

You can do whatever you believe you can do. It has been said there are no hopeless situations, only people who think hopelessly.

When you set challenging goals for yourself, and go on record and commit yourself to those goals, you think bigger and in effect stretch your mind, creating a better defined purpose and self-image. It's a practice I strongly recommend.

I have been using the estate tax approach and the simple four-page closer proposal since my first MDRT meeting. It helped me open cases and close cases. It just never seemed to miss. I wanted to be in my company's top twenty in 1964 and I was 17th. If you think you can—*you can.* I wanted to make the Million Dollar Round Table six years in a row to qualify for life membership. Six years later, 1967, I qualified for my life membership. If you think you can—*you can.*

I wanted to keep reaching higher and then I thought I had a chance to lead my company in 1966. So I worked harder and longer and when the year was over, I had paid for $7 million of new business. This earned me Runner-Up in volume—just $600,000 out of first place. I now had the confidence that I could write larger amounts by calling on *bigger businesses* and solving *bigger problems.* So I continued to use my estate tax approach and four-page closer and in 1970 I thought I could lead the company. So the big push was on for the year and I paid for $5.2 million in the last month only to finish *Runner-Up* for the *second time* to none other than my "idol," John O. Todd, who had just completed the now famous G.E. Case. My $9.3 million was second best *again.*

I was now *licking my wounds* and telling myself that if I had written $7 million and $9.3 million, if I worked smarter and solved bigger problems I could someday lead the NML. So I kept studying and working on larger prospects through *referred leads* and in 1972 I paid for $11.5 million with over $8 million in the month of May to finally *lead* the company.

If you think you can—you can! The feeling was great. I had momentum and I decided to go for it two years back to back. A year later I paid for $14.3 million— broke my previous year's record and was company leader for the second year in a row. This was such a thrill for me. I was determined to go for the third year in a row —break all Northwestern Mutual Life records. So I set my work schedule, organized my prospects and went to work. I also thought I would like to write the biggest single policy on one life that had ever been written in the NML. So I started *dreaming* about that and when the year ended, I had paid for over $24 million and with one policy of $10 million on one life.

If you can dream and *think you can—you can.*

The reason I keep using the estate tax approach and the four-page closer, which I was using when I spoke at the 40th MDRT Anniversary meeting in Lucerne, Switzerland and which I was still using when I spoke at the 50th Anniversary meeting of the MDRT in Atlanta, is that it just keeps *working* and *working* and *working*.

From the start 19 years ago with a card table in a spare bedroom, to the rented office with a part-time secretary, I have enjoyed the growth and development of a highly individualized operation, writing multi-millions each year. Because of my professional service concept, I have now a supporting staff of five highly qualified people, a large beautiful office complex, and a twin engine airplane that allows me to do business in a market area that covers eight western states. Continuity of service through a comprehensive staff arrangement has resulted in continued additional business from growing clients and the finest of referred leads. *If you think you can—you can!*

Face Up to Your Weaknesses

We all have our weaknesses. If we don't, we acquire them. As my approach started to work and the business started to grow, I became rather opinionated, less tolerant of the next person's viewpoint than I might have been. I have a good friend, Ed Frantz of Wichita, Kansas, a life insurance agent whose comments I reported in parts of the previous chapter. I'm proud I was able to help Ed work out some of his problems and achieve some of his goals. And I'm grateful that he helped me as well. After all, that's what friendship is all about.

Well, Ed's the kind of guy I find it worthwhile to listen to, observe, and emulate. He's a model of patience and tolerance. He listens hard. He examines himself.

Opening my mind, I learned from Ed the importance of being responsive to and pondering what the next person has to say. I learned not to be so opinionated, to respect and accept honest criticism.

Other people also have had a profound effect on me in different ways, helping me shore up my weaknesses and making my strengths even stronger. Listening to people, working together, learning from each other—it's a part of total development. There is more to the insurance business and the business of life than just pounding a beat, trying to sell another policy, chalk up another commission. None of us is perfect in this business. If you think you are perfect, that you have no weaknesses in need of correction, that you're not a candidate for self-improvement, it's only because you have imperfect standards.

Face the Hard Realities of Business Life

I think it is absolutely essential to keep in mind at all times—particularly if your clients are businessmen and professionals—that the main objective of business is profits, and that if you serve a businessman well you will help him increase the profitability of his enterprise. The same thing goes for yourself and for the business you run whether it consists of a one man operation or a large staff. It is what we refer to as the free enterprise system and I am one hundred percent in favor of it.

As strongly as I believe in service to others, in helping people in need, in contributing positively and constructively to the profession of which I'm so proud, I wouldn't want anyone to get the impression for one single moment that I'm running some kind of benevolent do-gooder operation. I thoroughly enjoy the lifestyle my profitable business has yielded, a beautiful home my wife, Connie, designed and decorated, a mountain home at Vail, my own office complex, private twin engine airplane, financial independence, and all the rest. Without a profit I could neither afford to contribute my time as I do in behalf of the industry and the ideals I espouse or, more importantly, continue to serve my clients.

Winston Churchill once said, "If you aim to profit, learn to please."

I think one thing stems from the other. One of the most wonderful discoveries I have ever made is that when you are in business to help, serve, and please, the profit comes as an automatic byproduct. And I would be the last one to sell profits short.

A Few Closing Thoughts

What does it all add up to—The Blessman Approach, the personal philosophy I'm trying to get across in this book?

It adds up to a system that worked.

I don't think there are many people in this business who struggled and skimped as much as I did, who were more scared, disillusioned, and discouraged than I was during the early months of my career. But I didn't quit and I'm proud of it. I worked and developed an approach where I could feel helpful and needed, where I could burrow down to the root of the problem and become part of the solution. I like to think that in the process I became a total person, something more than a salesman.

What I'm saying is that if it worked for me with my early limitations and ignorance, it can work for you too and the remaining chapters of this book will show you how.

I went through all kinds of torments and sacrifices to develop the approach described in this book. But once it was firmed up and honed, my business took off like a skyrocket. Today, 19 years later, just about every major commercial and professional enterprise that has been referred to me is now my client. And I have yet to have a person who has been referred to me refuse my offer of services. There have been several I declined after our initial meeting because if I can't represent a person with pride I do not want his business.

It is my strong conviction that if you follow the precepts and techniques described in this book you will never have to apologize for being in the life insurance business. You will never have to regard it as a stop gap until something more substantial comes along. You will be proud of it as I am, and your rewards both spiritual and financial will give you gratification and joy.

4.

STEPS TO SUCCESS —
PART I

Now, in getting down to the nuts and bolts of The Blessman Approach, let's forget about last year. Forget about yesterday. Let's talk about today and tomorrow.

It is easier to sell a businessman a hundred thousand dollar or a million dollar life insurance policy today than it was to sell him a ten thousand dollar policy five or ten years ago. *Because the large policy is so desperately and so clearly needed!* And so clearly affordable. That's the beauty of it. You don't have to worry about qualifying the affluent, successful businessman I'm talking about. You know in advance that he's qualified.

Hah!, you reply, that may be easy to say, but how do you do it? How do you go about selling a million dollar policy to a wealthy businessman?

The answer is so simple, it will make you blink. You sell a million dollar life insurance policy by *not selling* the policy. Instead you sell the client on his clear and undeniable need for the product and service you are offering him. In short, you don't walk into the client's office expecting to walk out with a contract. Does this sound paradoxical? It's not, as you will see.

Prime Key: The Development Effort

I've seen it time and again. The mistake the average agent keeps making is to imagine he can call on a businessman, chew the fat for an hour or two and sell him a life insurance policy that has some meaning and substance to it. I know the route because I've run it myself.

From what I've seen of the average run-of-the-mill insurance man, he understands a little bit about the client's problems and needs and a little bit about the product he's selling and how it can be a partial solution. Equipped with this inadequate knowledge and the ancient axiom about the law of percentages, he hopes the client will buy his package.

He stands up at the plate, takes a mighty blind swing at the ball, and if he's lucky enough to connect one time out of thirty, he races around the bases like a dog chasing his tail, neglecting to touch first, second, or third, hoping to score a home run before the client takes a second look to see what he's signed. Well, I can tell you one thing about the insurance business or any other business. You can't score a home run without tagging up on all bases.

No sir, it simply won't work that way. When it comes to selling that million dollar policy, the concept is as simple as I said, and it is virtually foolproof. But there's nothing easy about the procedure, and there's no way I know to get around the hard work. Nor would I want such a way if I could find it, because the work is an important part of the satisfaction and joy. I thrive on the work.

In a nutshell, the point I'm making is this. That big ticket sale doesn't just happen. *You have to set the stage for success.* You have to make a commitment to yourself and your clients and then carry it out. You have to provide *real* service, not lip service. You have to take a difficult problem, work out practical solutions to it, and boil it all down to simple terms the client will understand and appreciate. In the end, that's a major objective, to win the client's appreciation because he knows you're all for him and that you're helping him out of a problem. Once you achieve this objective, he'll be your client and, more important, your friend, for life.

Selling By the Book

One of the smartest moves I ever made, and one you can make too, was to buy a copy of a book entitled, "Your Estate Research Service." The findings appearing in this book were compiled by the Estate Research Institute, an independent statistical organization, from a survey of the court records of over 12,000 estates probated in all parts of the United States. (Three representative cases from the book are included as Exhibit I in Appendix.) The Estate Research Institute's address is P.O. Box 706, Aptos, California 95003. I took this guide and studied the various costs that have to be met when one dies—debts, inheritance taxes, estate taxes, legal fees and other costs of dying and transferring property.

This book was an education in itself. Its purpose is

to show, by means of authentic illustrations, what it costs to settle estates. Many people will receive money from your estate before your family receives what is left. Taxes, fees, debts and administration expenses—all these must be paid before an estate can be settled. A knowledge of what has happened to other estates is a valuable foundation on which to make plans for the protection of your own estate. Here is a direct quote from the book:

"Recent studies of court records reveal that three out of four estates lack sufficient cash to pay the estate settlement expenses. Money must be raised to meet these costs before the remaining assets can be distributed among the beneficiaries. This means forced sale of securities, real estate or business properties in 75% of today's estates and forced liquidation of assets usually results in heavy additional losses. These cash needs are to be met within six to nine months after death."

Armed with this book and a Federal 706 tax form and tax table, I started calling on businessmen who were successful. I simply asked them if they had ever seen the probate records of other successful businessmen like themselves. I asked them if they were aware of the high cost of dying. I would then sit beside them and read several of the estate settlement sheets.

The experience was an eye-opener for them, just as it had been for me at the outset. I started using this simple estate tax approach over 16 years ago, and I have never stopped since. It helped me to open and close cases. It just never seemed to miss because the logic and need are so obvious.

Help Wanted

In any case, the point I am making is this: When you

serve people honestly, responding when help is wanted and needed, the natural human reaction is appreciation. Give a person something he needs and, if nothing more, he will pay attention to you. And more often than not he will respond with friendship and gratitude.

Help is wanted everywhere you go. I see it every day of the year. What you have to do is sit down with people and get inside of them. Through communication you have to get to the root of their problems, and again through communication come up with solutions that will make their lives happier and more secure, and provide the peace of mind we all yearn for. Accomplish this and you will win a confidence and acceptance that can never be shaken.

I have yet to meet a successful business or professional man who was not deeply concerned about taxes, about seeking tax shelters for income and selecting investments that had tax advantages. Yet many of these very people fail to plan for the greatest tax burden of all, the one assessed when they die, the one involving United States Estate Tax Form 706.

Time and again I have placed a copy of this form in the hands of a businessman and asked if he knew what it was, if he had any idea of what happens to the estates of successful men at the time of their death. Nine out of ten admit they never thought of the problem although the perpetuity of their enterprise usually vaguely disturbs them.

I point out that every gross estate currently exceeding $120,000 and $175,000 in 1981 must file not in personal property, stocks and bonds, or real estate, but in cash. At this moment, I tell them, the hundred or so thousand in cash you could lay your hands on today seems like an impressive reserve. However, as you can see from this estate settlement book (see Exhibit I), the heirs of successful men quite often are required to come up with far more than this amount to meet the estate liquidity requirement. And what seems like an adequate reserve today may be wholly inadequate, two, five, or ten years from today as inflation takes its continuing bite.

The next step is to demonstrate to the businessman, using Form 706, how Uncle Sam will require a complete fair market value asset inventory of everything he owns and everything he owes. It is from this asset inventory that estate taxes are calculated. The tax table itself is right there on the form. It states, for example, that a $500,000 taxable estate will require $155,800 in cash, that a $750,000 taxable estate will take a tax bite of $248,300, and that a person with a million dollar taxable estate will have to get up $345,800 to satisfy the tax obligation.

Most people concentrate on the here and now, what is happening today, what's likely to happen tomorrow. They think only in terms of themselves on the scene. Very few wealthy men know what Form 706 is all about or that a huge amount of money will have to be shelled out by their heirs on demand shortly after their death. So the first step in The Blessman Approach is to make the individual you are trying to serve aware of this form and of what the future must inevitably bring. If he is willing to come to grips with this reality, and he almost invariably is, you can take it from there.

"Getting To Know You"

"Getting to know you," as the popular show tune goes, is an important part of The Blessman Approach. The last thought in my mind is to strut out a rate book or ask the prospective client for his business. After laying the groundwork, I let him know I am interested in him because he is successful and because I represent successful people in all walks of life.

I explain that it may be in his best interests to know what I do and how I operate. Even if we never do business together, he may gain some important insights and get some valuable information. I want him to see some of our credentials and the kind of service we perform. I say that if at some time you might want us to represent you and to explore your situation in depth, I would be delighted to do so because you're the kind of person we work with.

I extend an invitation for him to visit my office, to talk with our people, and view our operation first hand. I offer to fly him to Sterling. I want him to see our physical plant first hand and meet my staff.

I want him to know as much as possible about the all-encompassing financial services we offer. An informed client is the client we have.

I fly people into Sterling or they fly or drive on their own from all over the state and from other states, too. We talk about what information we will need to do the service job right, not only for me, the insurance agent, but for the other professionals as well. We explain what the attorney will need to fulfill his estate planning role, what the banker will have to know in the financial area, what information the accountant will require to properly analyze costs and determine potential tax liabilities.

I make clear my own role in collecting all of this data and sorting it out, getting together with the attorney, accountant, and banker to coordinate the estate planning and thinking, to integrate every action with a common objective in mind. I explain how the goal is to arrive at, not merely an insurance solution, but an overall action plan that will yield the greatest financial advantage, and how, after designing this long range plan, we will live with it and keep it current on a year-to-year basis.

Can you visualize how the pattern unfolds, how we are not in this business to make a one-shot quick sale, but to serve the client for the rest of his life?

These successful business and professional people are shrewd and sharp. They are quick to understand and appreciate the value of coordinating the whole financial effort, of working and thinking as a harmonious team instead of on a fragmented and segmented basis with one professional acting independently, and too often in ignorance, of the others.

There's something more. The people I serve are a very proud breed. They worked hard to get where they are and are fiercely possessive of what they have won. They want their sons, or daughters, or sons-in-law to carry on in the business if possible. They don't want their holdings sold off for peanuts, or sacrificed for the cash needed to meet estate tax obligations.

But most of them are so dynamic and busy, so highly involved in the day-to-day problems of running the business, and so very much alive, they've never given D-Day much thought.

Still they are intelligent enough and educable enough to be concerned when the point is hit home. And when the problem begins to unfold, what they want are fresh creative ideas. Nine out of ten times they will pose the key question themselves:

"How can I preserve and protect what I've earned? How can I keep the assets I worked hard for all of my life to acquire from going down the tax drain when I die?"

You see, no "sale" has to be made. The need speaks out for itself. All over this wonderful nation wealthy and successful people are searching for people like us to help them answer these questions. They're crying for someone who cares, someone who will take over and help define their problems and develop the solutions they need to solve these problems.

Qualifying Yourself

As you can see, qualifying the prospective client is no problem if you use The Blessman Approach because most successful businessmen are automatically qualified. They have the problem for which the agent is needed on the one hand, and on the other the resources to solve it. The trick is to qualify *yourself*, and in the final reckoning that's all that it takes.

This could not bear too much repetition. You qualify yourself by becoming a student of business. You access every source of knowhow you can. Billy Rose once said that the payoff in business is in direct ratio to the amount of specialized knowhow in the businessman's head.

The more savvy and knowledgeable you can become about business, taxes, law, and financial management, the more information you can assimilate that is readily applicable in the field, the more valuable you will be to the client, the greater your earning potential will be. Northwestern Mutual, along with most other companies, boasts a highly advanced and sophisticated training facility which has all of the factual information, forms, and documents one could require. I have always made the best possible use of my company's educational instruction and guides; it is one of my main sources of knowledge. I have even taken some of this material to the offices of accounting and law firms I deal with to assist them in their efforts to work more constructively for the client.

Knowledge is not only power, as Lord Bacon once

wrote; it generates credibility as well. Become a genuine expert in your field and clients will flock to your door. Nothing is more convincing or persuasive than knowhow. Knowhow inspires belief, trust, and respect. It qualifies you, the agent, as a problem solver. From that point on it is simply a matter of getting the problems and solutions together.

The Capital Transfer Concept

The businessman deals in specifics and facts. He understands the numbers that relate to his enterprise. He has little patience with vague generalities, and scare tactics turn him off.

Thus far you have provoked the prospective client's interest and stimulated his concern by presenting the estate conservation problems that face him. The task now is to relate the problem you presented and your method of solving it to his unique situation. Do this convincingly and you will command his attention as it was never commanded before.

The idea is to talk to him in his *language*. Don't talk insurance, talk business. Inventory, for example, is a word every businessman knows. When you explain the need for an inventory and preprobate of his assets, he will recognize its importance at once. I generally like to start off with an illustration he can relate to his own operation.

I happen to be located in a part of the country famous for its ranches and farms. As a case in point I often use the estate profile of a successful rancher, but the same approach would work as well for a manufacturing company, commercial enterprise, professional practice, or almost anyone else. Summarizing the rancher's estate, let us assume that his cash, real estate, live stock, machinery, outside investments, stocks and bonds, and life insurance on himself amount to a grand total of $2,233, 400. That is what he has accumulated in his lifetime. His current indebtedness is $233,400 showing a net worth of $2,000,000. (See Exhibit II in Appendix for itemized accounting.)

Using this figure we can determine what the approximate death taxes and transfer costs would be. The debts of $233,400 would be paid by his executors at the time of his death. Now let's add in $11,500 for funeral costs, and legal and administration expenses of $48,500. Assume his wife survives him. The full marital deduction is available. The Federal estate tax of $267,343 and state death taxes of $19,757 would be due. This amounts to a total cash requirement of $580,500 that the rancher's heirs will have to produce out of his cattle and machinery, prime real estate, stocks and bonds, and other assets within six to nine months after his death.

Assuming that the generation of this massive cash sum was not planned during his lifetime, the executor will be faced with a number of options. Let's assume that the need was exactly $200,000 for this illustration. One is to mortgage some of the real estate. To generate cash of $200,000, perhaps $300,000 of prime property would have to be put up as collateral. If the executor succeeded in getting a 20-year mortgage with a 9% interest rate, interest alone for the first year would be $18,000. On top of that, a 5% principal payout would amount to $10,000 for the first year and every year thereafter. It's also important to note that the principal would have to be paid with *after-tax dollars*. Assuming that the estate already is in the 50% ordinary income tax bracket, it must earn $20,000 before income tax to have the $10,000 left over for the annual principal payment. Therefore, it would require 9% interest plus 5% principal or a total of 14% of the $200,000 capital needed to pay the bill—to service the new debt.

If this option seems too expensive, the executor may wish to consider selling a piece of the prime property to generate the cash that is needed. As likely as not, this would have to occur under forced sale conditions. If the market is poor at the time and the economic outlook not very encouraging, the widow and heirs would have to sacrifice for a fraction of its worth what the rancher took a lifetime to build. What is more, there are usually overlooked hidden costs when assets are sold. If prime property is sold to generate $200,000 of cash, that $200,000 of after-tax capital instantly disappears from the estate. Even at a minimum 7% interest per year, it would amount to an income loss of $14,000 annually or $140,000 for 10 years and $280,000 over a 20-year period in income alone and the $200,000 principal is lost forever.

As experience only too well testifies, mortgaging property or selling property is a very expensive way to meet the tax requirement for cash. By proper planning during one's lifetime, an executor would not have to resort to this method. One of the most powerful financial tools used in proper estate planning is life insurance, properly drawn up and arranged. Applied to this purpose, life insurance is designed to meet the estate tax cash need before it arises.

Let's assume this same rancher planned ahead and had $200,000 of life insurance properly owned. Assuming the same set of numbers, a $200,000 whole life policy purchased at age 45 would make the required cash available instantly. The question is, how much did it cost? The figures I will use are from a mutual company and reflect dividends based on the current scale, not an estimate or guarantee of future results.

For a $200,000 policy purchased at age 45, the ten-year average annual net premium is $5,000. This is 2.5%

of the $200,000. The average annual guaranteed cash value of $4,600 is 2.3% of the $200,000 policy. The difference between the premium and guaranteed cash value amounts to $400, the average annual cost of the policy in addition to the net cost of the money. What this boils down to is two-tenths of one percent of the $200,000, and here's how it works.

Each year the insured pays the $5,000 net premium out of his asset inventory. But what is important to remember is that he isn't spending this money; $4,600 of the $5,000 goes into the policy's guaranteed cash value. It only costs him $400 a year plus the net after tax cost of the use of the money. Over 20 years the average guaranteed cash value is returned to the policy amounting to an average annual gain of $298. In effect, the only real cost of the $200,000 is the average net cost of the money less the gain in the policy.

How does the life insurance option compare with the other options discussed? This is the most compelling aspect of The Blessman Approach. A 20-year mortgage at 9% plus a 5% principal payment brings the total cost to 14%. What we are comparing this against is a two-tenths of one percent cost plus the average net cost of the money on a whole life policy on a 10-year average. Or, after 20 years, only the average net cost of the money less the gain in the policy.

Comparing this option to outright sale, there we lost a precious asset forever, plus earnings of at least 7% on a year-to-year basis.

Basically, this is the Capital Transfer Concept of selling large amounts of life insurance to successful people. Applying this concept I personally sold millions of dollars of cash value life insurance. There is no reason I can think of why you can't do the same thing.

Get That Master Plan Started

I think you would have to go a pretty long way before finding an enterprise or objective that failed as a result of overplanning. From every effort that suffered from overplanning, I would guess you could come up with a thousand or more that failed because they weren't planned properly.

It applies to building bridges. It applies to estate settlement. I could cite case after case where substantial estate tax costs that could easily have been avoided were incurred because the businessman or professional man neglected to plan ahead during his lifetime. This isn't wild speculation; the probate records from coast to coast are on hand to prove this contention. Nor are the losses in dollars alone. If you begin to consider the emotional upheaval—disruption of young peoples' college careers, lost control of the business because of insufficient liquidity, the bank's line of credit withdrawal—that is a byproduct of inadequate planning, it's enough to produce tears of distress.

Estate planning was once referred to by a Price Waterhouse senior partner as an "executive blindspot." Two weeks of solid work on his estate, he remarked, "may be worth more to an executive than his financial gains of the past 10 or 15 years."

I can say from experience that taking advantage of existing tax laws and opportunities—the fully qualified marital deduction, the $3,000 annual gift tax exclusion, proper trust planning—avoidance of joint tenancy ownership, buy-sell agreement, business continuation arrangements, capital transfer provisions, and other strategies—a businessman can save from 25% to 45% or earn up to a maximum of 70% of his holdings.

When this is explained simply and logically, with

evidence submitted to support what you say, nine out of ten successful businessmen will respond with concern, realizing that here is a matter they should have attended to a long time ago. Recognizing the importance of planning in running his business, a businessman will understand its importance in protecting the assets he worked so long and so hard to acquire.

I am talking about continuous year-to-year planning, the only kind that is meaningful. It's not enough to do a good thorough job today, present the client with a neatly tied package and say, "Here it is, Mr. Jones, your needs are now all taken care of." Because they're not. A year or three from today, with inflation's continuing toll, with all the pending tax reforms, legislative changes, and shifting family conditions and requirements, nothing will stay constant for long. I have learned in this profession that the only way you can do a superlative job for the client is to start planning today and continue planning for as long as you serve him. This is the message I constantly hammer across, a message the smart and successful businessman will respond to.

It is never too early for a successful person to shape his course for the future. The time to work up the plan is *before* that partnership agreement is signed, before the corporation is formed, before the will is created, before any piece of paper is signed that will arrange funding, divide profits, commit assets, or incur financial liabilities.

And that's where *you* come into the picture.

Leads: The Natural Approach

Referrals are the building blocks of an insurance man's business. I have learned over the years that the best way to develop leads is to let them develop themselves. Naturally. Logically. I've also learned that natural lead development is an automatic byproduct of helpful and dedicated service.

In business, once you show that you have the capability and savvy to help people, you'd be surprised how fast the word gets around. A few months ago, an oil millionaire in his sixties walked into my office and dumped an armload of papers on my desk—legal documents, contracts, insurance policies. "Okay," he said, "you're so blasted smart, let's see if you are as good as they say you are." He turned and walked out of my office.

A friend of his for whom we worked had told him about our organization and what we were doing.

Another time I was having lunch with a client and we were joined by two other men. After chatting a while one of them said, "Hey, would you consider coming to Denver to take a look at our operation? I'm taking in a junior partner, selling him fifty percent of the business. I think you may be able to help us."

He was the head of an engineering firm of consultants. He knew who I was. My client had filled him in beforehand.

I flew to Denver and sat down with his accountant and attorney. I helped to formulate and coordinate a plan that integrated his personal financial planning and his business assets. I've been serving him ever since.

This kind of thing happens time and again. It's like a snowball rolling downhill. Once you get started and begin proving your worth and gathering momentum, the leads tend to develop themselves, and a million dollar lead develops just as easily and naturally as a $5,000 one.

Let the Leads Come to You. One thing I can tell you: I won't call on a person until I know enough about him and am referred by a client who is satisfied with my services.

Does that sound smug? I don't mean it to. Hell, all I'm saying is that when you let the leads come to you, it saves a lot of valuable time. And once you get rolling with The Blessman Approach, you'll no longer have to scrounge around knocking on doors.

My clients are successful people who live and work and play with other successful people. I believe in them and they believe in me. If I wish to make contact with a successful person I will make arrangements to do so with my client. Most often I will go with my client to pick up the referral. We will have lunch or play tennis or golf or do something of common interest. My initial objective is not to sell life insurance but to meet and get to know the referral on a social, personal, and generally casual basis.

At some point during this period my client will probably let the referral know that I have been handling his affairs for the past six or eight years.

He may make some such remark as, "Watch out for this guy; he'll get all of your money." Or, "Here's my expensive insurance agent."

We spend very little time talking business. Somewhere during the conversation I may say, "I would sure like to come see your office—or your medical clinic or feed yard or ranch—one of these days. I've been out that way a number of times."

He is apt to reply, "I'd love to have you. Why don't you give me a call when it's convenient and I'll show you around."

A few days later I'll call him and that's how the ball starts to roll. Of course, a lot of time has been spent behind the scene probing and checking up on the person and his business. But up to this point we haven't even discussed life insurance.

When I visit him, we'll start discussing business and I'll learn more about his problems, needs, and concerns, how he thinks and feels and what made him successful. I don't have to tell you this is something he is justifiably proud of and enjoys talking about. Eventually I lead him into the sales-service relationship by inquiring about his attorney, banker, CPA, and doctor, and I find out who has been selling him insurance, both personal and business, and what kind of protection he has.

I ask about the other professional people who are serving him and about the actual results they achieved. Does he have a current will properly drafted? Has he set up any trusts for benefit of his family? If so, what are the terms? Has he prepared a current asset inventory reflecting today's fair market value? How do he and his wife hold title to these assets?

And as you can see, by now we are right into the heart of it in a friendly business-like way.

Building a Team for the Client

During my early days in the business I would hear agents complain time and again, "Any time I get a sale under way, it is killed by an accountant or lawyer." The way they talked one would think that these people were their enemies.

I couldn't accept that as being a fact. I decided that if I was going to work with these successful businessmen on their problems, I would be coming into contact with other professionals who served them as well, and that the last thing I wanted was to have these men as my enemies. The best way to win a person over as a friend is to be open and honest with him. So the first thing I do after arranging to work for a client is to visit the law firm, accounting office, and bank that serves him, and introduce myself to these people.

By now they all know me, of course, but in the early days I would say, "Mr. Attorney (or Mr. Accountant, or Mr. Banker), I don't want you guys over here wondering what that Blessman is up to. I don't practice law," I added, "I don't set up trusts, and I don't give tax advice. I'm not qualified in these areas and I don't pretend that I *am*. But I *am* qualified to design plans and make provisions that will conserve the client's assets, integrate his financial planning, and protect his business and family in the event of his death."

"Well now," these people replied, "we'll be glad to work with you on that basis. We never before have had anyone approach us in this manner. We usually find out about the life insurance after the fact."

So, as you can see, the professional way to do business is to establish relationships like this in advance. And it is well worth the effort. The way it worked out, some of my biggest boosters are attorneys, accountants, and bankers. We work in close and harmonious liaison with some of the most important and prestigious law offices and accounting firms in the state.

An indication of how well this approach is received is the invitations I get from time to time to address Bar Association meetings on the subject of what I refer to as interprofessional relationships and the value of fostering them.

Nor are these professionals willing to work with me

because they like my personality or the way I part my hair. Here's an agent who takes an open and cooperative approach, they reason. They are convinced I'm not trying to lure away their clients or steer them down the wrong path. On top of that I let them know I will be making suggestions to clients that involve the need for wills, trusts, buy-and-sell agreements, and all kinds of tax and legal advice. And they know these are things their professional ethics won't permit them to promote. They realize that my objective of bringing them and the client together so that we can exchange ideas and offer mutual inputs will benefit everybody concerned, primarily the client.

Leveling Upward

In chapter two I talked about Ed Frantz, another Northwestern Mutual agent and a very close friend of mine. I stated, if you will recall, that at the outset Ed was quite negative about the transferability of The Blessman Approach, convinced at the time he couldn't write more than a million or so dollars worth of business each year. As I said in conclusion, Ed is now up to over $7 million and climbing, and one reason for his success is that he learned the art of leveling upward.

In the beginning he was gun shy at approaching businessmen and professionals in the upper income brackets. But one of the things he found out is that the fellow earning $200,000 a year is as easy to reach as the one earning $15,000, and the guy who owns the operation is as easy to reach as the people who work for him. What's more, the individuals in the top echelons are the ones with the greatest need for asset conservation and the greatest need to have their financial and estate affairs put in order, and are the most educable people I know.

The trick in leveling upward is to make the transition so many agents are fearful of trying because they don't feel comfortable approaching highly successful and prosperous men. What if they ask me something I can't answer, they reason? What if I make a fool of myself?

Why should you, if you do your homework in advance?

From what I have seen, the only way to feel comfortable is to get in there and do it. Break down those mental barriers that exist nowhere but inside your head. Get that first experience under your belt, and when you see how good and satisfying it is, you won't be able to wait for the second. I know of nothing that hinders progress so much as fear of the unknown and unexpected. In identifying and helping to solve the client's problem you will be dissipating that fear. And I have yet to see any man who made another man feel embarrassed while he was in the process of helping him.

5.

STEPS TO SUCCESS —
PART II

I don't think I could stress strongly enough the importance of working as hard as you can to understand the technical aspects of estate planning and financial management, the legal and tax implications, the insurance options and forms that relate to your service. But if you imagine that's all there is to it, you're still a long way from reality.

The burning essence of The Blessman Approach is working with, through, and for people.

Even if you were the most savvy tax expert or financial wizard in the world, you couldn't climb to the top in this profession unless you had what it takes to make people believe in you as a person and desire your friendship.

Perform Like an Executive Vice President

The typical executive vice president in most large corporations has a good overall knowledge of the business and industry. He is bright and imaginative. He possesses insights and a deep understanding of his company's motivations and goals. A well paid manager, he usually reports directly to the president. And chances are he has enough savvy and smarts to put him in line for the chief executive officer's job when the time for succession comes due.

But in most cases, more than any other single factor, what makes him so valuable to the organization is his ability to get people to work with him, to resolve human problems and conflicts, bring key executives together in a concentrated thrust towards a common objective, stimulate cooperation and teamwork.

The executive VP usually knows better than anyone else on the team that, as Longfellow once said, "All your strength is in union. All your danger is in discord."

The toil we are talking about—and it is joyful toil indeed—is the kind that is shared by a team of professionals—accountants, attorneys, bankers, agents—who, ideally, work together in harmony in the client's best interest.

That's where you come into the picture, and where you must function as a well coordinated—and coordinating—executive VP.

The Most Important Step of All

No step you could take is more vital to making The Blessman Approach—or any other approach you could name—succeed than developing the ability to get people to work together amiably and harmoniously.

An old Indian saying states that, "When brother stands with brother, a war is already half won."

I can recall at least one situation in my experience, and it is typical of so many others, where two brothers who were prospective clients did not stand together and where a skilled coordinator was needed to keep the show on the road and to keep it from folding.

In this big ranching operation, both brothers were honorable men, but they suffered a conflict of interest; their positions were diametrically opposed. As I remember it, we were seated in the ranch office together; the brothers, their attorney, their accountant, and myself. On a preliminary basis, we were attempting to plan for the future, discussing a tentative buy-sell agreement. One of the brothers let me know quite bluntly that he didn't know for sure at this point if he was interested in life insurance or not.

"That's all right," I told him. "I'm not sure either. I don't even know if you're qualified."

I used this opportunity to ask, "Mr. Attorney, will his being qualified or not make a difference in the way you draft the buy-sell agreement?"

"It most certainly will," he replied.

The strategy, you can see, is: 1. To put him on record; 2. To find common ground we can work on; 3. Let him know I respect his opinion and take his participation for granted; 4. Ensure him I have no intentions of trying to horn in on his bailiwick.

The same approach applies to other professionals as well. At another point I interjected, "What about the tax aspects, Mr. Accountant? Will this create any problems?"

I don't offer tax advice or legal opinions, nor do I pretend to have expertise in these areas, and I want these men to know it.

What I do is coordinate. I try to make the group function as a team, every member playing his own unique position. To coordinate effectively it is essential to create an environment where goodwill and cooperation prevail, where all parties have confidence and faith in each other.

A little later the inevitable question was raised: "In the event of death, how much money will be needed to meet the estate tax cash requirement?"

"Over two hundred thousand dollars," the accountant replied.

"Well now," I said, "if all the income-producing assets are tied up as we discussed, where is that cash going to come from?"

I waited for the answer I knew I wasn't going to get. It gave everyone in that room, and the brothers in particular, something to think about. A clause in the proposed agreement was supposed to give the older brother a substantial income each month. The younger brother looked worried.

"Hey listen," he said, "in the event of your death, if we're going to plow all that money we've been talking about back into the business, and if I have to hire someone to take your place, we won't be able to afford to shell out all of that income."

There was an uncomfortable silence.

"All right," I cut in, "let's look at the situation realistically . . . ."

Get the drift? It's a charged and highly personal problem. There is a clear, and potentially explosive, conflict of interest. We have to deal with issues of crucial concern to both brothers. Decisions must be made that involve accounting, legal, and tax aspects of the business. How can you make such decisions in the clients' best interests without all parties and all experts present and operating in good faith as a team? And how can you achieve this objective without first properly setting the groundwork?

You can't.

Function Like a Family Member

Voltaire once wrote, "Judge a man by his questions rather than by his answers."

The most successful professional people I know— lawyers, bankers, accountants, doctors, insurance agents—are the ones who ask the right questions about the right subjects at the right time.

Differences, conflicts, and squabbles take place in the best of families. The old head of a thriving family feedlot business, a man I had been serving for 12 years, recently told me, "Lyle, my boys don't always get along the way I'd like them to. They have their rough times and problems. If anything ever happens to me, and one day it's inevitable, I want you to promise me that you will stay between them. I want to count on you as a stabilizing influence, to grab ahold of them and make sure they do the right thing."

I sincerely promised to do that. He has enough confidence in me to know that I think and function like a member of the family. This knowledge gives him a measure of peace and contentment, and it gives me a warm and wonderful feeling.

To function like a family member you have to know the family from the inside out. You have to understand and sympathize with their aspirations and goals. You have to know their strengths and their weaknesses.

Which brings us back to the questions. You need a lot of very personal and confidential information, the kind you get only when the family's faith in you is complete.

From the head of the family, I had to know: What are your objectives in life? How do you see your children? What about your son who will soon be coming out of college? Will he go into the business with you, or seek a career in medicine or law? What about your daughter and son-in-law? What hopes and plans for them do you have?

What about your wife? Does she understand the business? Would she be able to manage it in your absence? Would you want her to own the business when you are gone? How does *she* feel about it? Would it be better to have her interests pulled out, the money set up in a trust so that she would be provided for without all of the headaches and responsibilities that go hand in hand with a business? What about your key employees? What provisions do you want made for them?

Does your wife come from a family of any potential inheritance? If so, what effect would that have on your plans? Do you have any potential inheritance or obligations? Do you have any aged relatives who are dependent on you? What about your brothers and sisters?

What are your hopes for the business? Where would you like it to be 10 years from today? If your daughters decide to come back, is the business set up to take care of them and their husbands? If they wish to participate in the business and build homes nearby, do you have enough land to provide for this? Would it be a good idea to buy another quarter? Do you want to set up specific units or operations of the business for your sons to take over?

You gather all of this information and more, not only for yourself, but for the entire financial management team. The main idea in good business planning and estate management is not to simply minimize the death costs and provide for paying the taxes, but to fulfill the client's objectives and desires in the most practical, economical, and harmonious way. The desires come first, the tax considerations second.

To accomplish this goal as a planner you must expose the client's inner core. You must operate in effect like a dentist. You don't start drilling away until you take a good set of x-rays to see where the cavity is.

Go Out of Your Way To Prove That You Care

Most people you deal with aren't really that much concerned about *you*. They want to sell you a car, a piece of equipment, a policy. They want to draw up your documents or keep your books. They want to drill your teeth or treat your illness. But as a person you rarely get a second thought.

To make The Blessman Approach succeed, you must reverse this philosophy. In my book clients are more than clients; they're people. More important than that, they are friends. I worry about their fortunes and health. If they have problems I want to know about them so that I can share them. When they're in trouble I want to give them a hand. If you are unable to feel this way about people, The Blessman Approach is not for you.

If there is one trouble with business, with the country, with the world, it is that too many people simply do not give a damn.

A couple of years ago a rancher client of mine was the victim of a massive flood in our area. At the peak of it his cattle lot was under several feet of water and rising. The way I felt, it could have been my very own lot. I was right in there with him, moving out 20,000 head of cattle. Some of them got caught in irrigation ditches. We had to get cables and winches. We had to get down there and tie the cable around their legs so that we could winch them out of those places.

I worked all through the night alongside of a rancher who was unable to swim and was scared to death he would drown. Debris floated all over the place. The power lines were down so that imminent danger of electrocution existed. At one point I had to dive and swim under water to unlatch the gates because I knew how they worked. We literally drove those cattle out of there, right through the town to the high country beyond.

When we finally got them all out I flopped down on a bed some place and slept for two or three hours. Later on I was back again with a big Caterpillar front end loader and we started cleaning the pens and moving out the debris. It took us more than four days to get the place back into shape, into a condition where we could put in some feed and bring the cattle back down.

I'm not saying this boastfully but matter-of-factly. I never thought of my own skin. Thoughts of being bone-weary never occurred to me. I simply plunged in and helped to do what I knew had to be done because a friend was in trouble. And herein lies the root and foundation of The Blessman Approach.

Too many people pay lip service to caring. They say that they care, but don't prove it.

How can you prove it? By coming through in a

pinch. But pinches don't always occur. The idea is to prove that you care about people whether you are with them or not. I will call a client from Los Angeles or Dallas, simply wanting to know how things are going. Is the new system working out as you hoped? How's the little guy? Is he feeling better today? What did the doctor say?

Is there anything I can do?

Sometimes there's not a thing you can do, but offering can make a great deal of difference. After all, in a good close knit family, isn't that how members act?

Serve as the Client's Unlicensed Analyst

The same way a dentist wouldn't be much of a professional if he took a quick superficial look at your teeth and started to drill, so you wouldn't be much of an agent if you focused on a single insurance need and disregarded the other factors. Yet that's what the average life insurance man seems to think estate planning is all about. He zeroes in on a handful of facts relating to the financial situation at death and is all set to pull out his forms and start writing. It's no wonder so many policies are improperly planned and drawn up.

To do the best possible job for a client, you have to know and understand him the way a good psychiatrist understands a patient after long months of psychoanalysis. You have to get inside of the man. In attempting to do this I have found it very helpful over the years to let him get inside of you as well. My clients know, for example, that I have four youngsters and a wife I've been married to for 20 years.

Do you get the idea? My clients know most of what I've been through to get where I am. They know that

I've stood alone bucking the system. That I know what it is to be lonely, that I understand what it means to be scared, because most of them have been there themselves. It's the kind of talk people can identify with and respond to.

When you expose your own inner self you encourage others to do the same thing, to relate to you not only as a businessman, but as a human being as well.

Climbing the Mountain Step by Step

Summing up, the foundation of The Blessman Approach is:

1. Getting to know the client as well as you might know a close and loved family member and,

2. Armed with this knowledge, laying the groundwork and preparing the environment in a way that will enable you to coordinate all professional planning and thinking with the client's best personal and financial interests in mind.

Pounding home these critical points, I like to use the mountain climbing analogy. When a skilled climber goes up a sheer cliff driving steel pins above him each step of the way, he makes certain that each pin is absolutely solid and securely imbedded. Making your way up the ascending precipice of success is pretty much the same process. The idea is to keep that steel pin in mind and make sure you drive it home so that it is solid and secure and supports your whole weight thousands of feet above the canyon floor. Think of each step as a step toward your goal that your very life may depend on.

Making your way up that mountain, the temptation always exists to minimize one of the steps. But all it takes is a single inadequately secured pin to bring you crashing back down to the bottom.

What follows are the main building blocks that make up the foundation of The Blessman Approach. Like the pins a mountain climber uses to make his ascent up a formidable peak, all it takes is one weak block to make the structure collapse. These simple basic guidelines will constitute your driving force and your strength as you slowly attempt to scale that peak.

What you will read are simple and basic truths which, precisely because they're so basic, are so often overlooked or ignored. The idea in reading and examining these guidelines is to adopt the attitude of a person who never before read a book. Imagine that you are seeing these words and absorbing these thoughts for the very first time. Take a completely new and fresh look. Try to recapture the attitude you had as a child, the one that provoked you to burst out with a "Wow!" or "Oh boy!" when a simple truth was exposed.

In that spirit, consider the kind of person you will have to be—not imitate or pretend to be, but actually BE—to master the art and skill of working with, for, and through people to help them achieve their objectives and to achieve your own in the process.

Infuse yourself and others with optimism.

I talked earlier about the need to spread sunshine. Never is it more important to apply this axiom than when you are engaged in a team effort with others. It has been said that the same rain that saves the optimist's lawn, makes the pessimist's weeds grow faster.

Your attitude when you are functioning as part of a team, and particularly when you are functioning as the coordinator of that team, can determine the outlook of each member you work with. Just as all team members must work as a unit to get the job done right, so must they think as a unit to establish the conviction that the job can and will be done right.

The wise person knows that the likelihood of his seeing through the veils and mysteries of life to the absolute truth at all times is slim. Most of us must settle for some kind of hypothesis on which to base our actions, an organizing principle we can subscribe to even though we can never know in any absolute mathematical way whether we are taking the best course or not. I'm talking about the kind of working hypothesis that makes you *feel* you are right. You drive your car up to a bridge over a small river. The bridge looks well built and solid. Still, bridges have collapsed in the past.

But this one you trust. It *feels* right. So instead of waiting for an engineering analysis of load and stress, you push down on the accelerator and drive across it. We make judgments of this kind every day.

An optimistic outlook, in my opinion, is that kind of hypothesis. You work on the premise that the world is basically good, and that things will get better instead of worse. You believe that people are basically decent if you give them a chance. The pessimist goes on the assumption that things are more bad than good, that the next guy is out to get him, that the evil forces in this world will prevail.

Pondering these conflicting views, I let my mind drift back to the beginnings of recorded history, to the countless rising and falling civilizations from Egypt and Greece to Rome, the Middle Ages, and recent times. And I think about the average person such as myself living anywhere in the world but, since I am an American, mainly in terms of this country. And I say to myself, "There were many fascinating periods in history, but I honestly can't think of any time I'd rather live than right now. In fact, I think this is the most interesting and exciting time to be alive in the entire history of mankind."

Now that's optimism and it's well grounded in fact. We're making continuous progress, aren't we? The forces of good are prevailing. In many important ways, the world is better than it has ever been in the past. I can believe that, and I don't have to strain to believe it. And believing it, I can believe in people as well.

But too many of us have negative attitudes. Understandably. Nothing worthwhile is easy to obtain. We can see roadblocks and setbacks ahead of us if that's what we look for. Few battles are won without disappointments and losses.

Too many people are too easily discouraged, and one of your chief jobs as coordinator is to accentuate the positive, to replace, "It's too hard," with "We sure as hell can do it!" And I have found that to be true time and again. Assuming that the proper precautions were taken—the necessary knowledge acquired, the essential harmony and goodwill promoted—the job almost always seems to come out right.

In my experience I have found that on the one hand it is important never to underestimate the power of a positive attitude, while on the other taking care never to use optimism as a substitute for hard work.

*Don't forget to be pleasant.

It's so easy to get caught up in your own little problems and hassles. You're irritated by a minor physical ailment. Charley neglected to call as he promised. That package you were supposed to get didn't arrive. You received a "no" when you expected a "yes."

Hey, that's all part of living. For every minus you can think up two plusses. The trouble is if we become too much engrossed in our own little problems, become irritable as a result, *and show our irritation to others*, it tends to multiply and backfire.

I try to make it a point to never forget that I'm in the business of communicating with people. The simple fact of the matter is that if you want people to respond warmly and amiably to you, that's the attitude you have to get across to them.

Think for a moment. When people conjure up your face in their minds do they see a sour grumpy picture with the mouth turned down, or smiling features filled with warmth and goodwill. Do they think, "Hey, there's good old Jim; I always enjoy seeing that guy," or, "Uh, uh, here comes Jim again; I'm gonna make myself scarce"?

It's so basic, you wonder how so many people miss it. If you act pleasantly, you will make others feel and act pleasantly in return. People who act pleasant get along better with people.

Give it some thought. How pleasant have you been lately? How much of the day do you spend frowning and surly; how much do you spend radiating warmth and goodwill? How much would it actually take to erase that frown of self-concern and replace it with a smile that will brighten the other guy's day as well as your own? Not a phoney, make believe smile. A real smile you believe in.

Try to see the good side of people.

Did you ever stop to think that the same guy who grumbles and grunts when he sees you may go out of his way to help somebody in need? Or that the person you impulsively judge to be a cutthroat or cheapskate may give generously to his favorite charity? Or that the individual who appears to be discourteous and brusque may have just experienced a setback he's unable to hide?

It's so easy to jump to conclusions based on somebody's single action or superficial behavior. Let's look at the human condition realistically. There's good and evil in all of us. We all make mistakes and misjudgments. Each of us in his time has done one thing or another he's ashamed of. But I honestly believe that the overwhelming majority of us are more plus than minus, that given a tenth of a chance we would do the thing that is basically decent and right.

The fact is, as the renowned cellist Pablo Casals once pointed out, "We're all leaves on a single tree."

We're all part of the same human race, struggling toward the fulfillment we seek, losing ground one day, picking it up the next.

Most of us are learning each day and reaching out to learn more. We are each of us part of so many great and wonderful things that are happening. If we stumble and fall now and then, so what? It's only par for the course because, being human, we're fallible.

The idea is to keep this in mind and not judge people impulsively. If you must judge them, give them the benefit of the doubt, try to see their good side instead of their bad. I discovered long ago that if you look for the good you will find it. Focus on the positive aspects of a person's personality and character and you will for one thing bring out the best in him, and for another, inspire the goodwill and harmony that *you* will need to succeed.

*Act the same way with everyone.

If you never tried this, you may find it a hard assignment to fill. You will have to examine your behavior from a new and different perspective. If you can achieve what I'm after, your energies will be greater and the impact of your personality more forceful than ever before.

Assess yourself honestly and objectively. Are you the same person when talking with the guy who mows your lawn as you are at a cocktail party being held by your town's social leaders? Do you use the same natural words, tone of voice, gestures? Do you walk the same, talk the same, and smile the same smile? Or do you tailor your behavior to each special occasion adjusting to the notion that this is how you ought to, or are expected to, act? Do you speak and act like a phoney?

This is a terrific problem in human relations. It's always easier to see the next person than it is to see ourselves. But unless you master the art of viewing and assessing yourself, you run the terrible danger of being pegged as insincere and pretentious by other people who view you.

One good way to overcome this danger is not to take yourself so seriously. Laugh at yourself once in a while. It's excellent therapy. If someone laughs at you, try laughing with them instead of feeling insulted.

I have found that an excellent test to conduct is to ask of yourself: "Would I be the same person, talking the same, acting the same, if I were on stage addressing a thousand people as I would be with an audience of one?"

If you can respond affirmatively to this, you're a natural genuine person and people will respond to you warmly. If you cannot respond affirmatively, you can train yourself to do so.

The first time I was invited to speak before a large

audience was at Northwestern Mutual's annual meeting
after my first really good year when I sold seven million
and stood number two in the company. John Todd, an insurance industry great who had about 40 years' experience behind him, was number one on the roster. I
was honored to have second place, although I've since
discovered I like first even more.

The annual meetings were always quite formal,
rather serious and proper, right out of the old school
text. When I was introduced and came out on the stage
of the old Riverside Theatre in Milwaukee, I found
myself face to face with four thousand people and bright
lights that blinded and dazed me. Then I said, "Holy
cow! You know, this place sure would hold a lot of hay."

Well now, I suppose that's just about as corny as
humor can get. But it wasn't for one minute calculated. I
hadn't thought it up backstage. It was a very natural
reaction, a farm boy's sense of the biggest building he
had ever seen somehow being related to the biggest
building he ever knew in the past, a barn. So it just came
out.

Well, people started to chuckle and then started to
laugh. And as the laughter gathered momentum, the audience started to roar. The trustees of the company were
sitting there along with heads of major corporations
from all over the country, and they began to roar with
the loudest of them.

After the meeting a high level company officer said
to me, "Young man, I'd like to shake your hand. You introduced a breath of fresh air that was long overdue."

I suppose it's easier for a country boy to have that
warm natural quality that's so appealing to people, to be
himself whatever the circumstances or audience. But

I've heard some wonderful speakers in our industry who are from big cities, from all kinds of ethnic and social backgrounds, and have a fabulous rapport with their audiences because they simply are what they are and they don't take themselves too seriously.

I can state from experience that it is a quality worth striving for. Achieve it, and you will be amazed at the results and at how much easier it will be to get people to work for you and with you.

Never waver off course.

Under The Blessman Approach, the "what's-in-it-for-me?" factor takes care of itself.

So many insurance agents breeze into a prospective client's office or home and first thing pull out a legal pad and begin throwing a battery of canned, memorized questions at the man. Good grief! What does that say to a person? It tells him that in your eyes he's no more than a model or type and that all you're doing is collecting statistics. The canned approach fails to recognize the man's individuality. It doesn't take his personal needs, hopes, and goals into consideration. And yet this is precisely the information we need if we expect to coordinate his family and financial aims and affairs.

The first thing you have to train yourself to do, Mr. Agent, is to leave that yellow pad in your briefcase. Don't take it out until you know your client so well that taking it out is a natural and logical course of action. Start by sitting down across from him, looking him in the eye, and talking as one man to another. If you can't do that, try to find out why. What is it that makes you want to lean on a crutch instead of relying on your instincts and knowledge? What is it that makes you want to depersonalize the interview when the very opposite is what you should be trying to achieve?

Ask questions? Absolutely! You won't get to know your man until you do. But ask questions about where he's been, where he's going, what he wants to do. Find out what's important to him. Search out his purposes and beliefs. Ask the kind of questions that will encourage him to respect you, to like you, to place his faith and confidence in your motivations and skill.

Ask questions, whether you're alone with the client, or in a room with his accountant, attorney, and banker, with one objective in mind:

How can I help *him?* Not me, HIM!

Concentrate on this and your ends will take care of themselves. What can I do to save him money, make his life easier, give him more peace of mind? How can I help him plan and coordinate his family and business affairs in a way that will fulfill his goals and needs most economically and beneficially? This, after all, is what service and friendship are all about. If you keep to this course, you cannot help but succeed.

6.

STEPS TO SUCCESS — PART III

I have heard patience defined as the ability to idle your motor when you feel like stripping your gears. A great many agents I know are not only stripping their gears but burning out their engines in the process.

In previous chapters I touched on the importance of taking your time and playing it cool. It's the only way I know to serve a client thoroughly and well and serve yourself as you do so. Unfortunately, that's not the way nine out of ten insurance agents view our profession. They think strictly in terms of the one or two interview sale, the fast close, the quick kill. Hey, I can think of no surer way than this attitude to undermine The Blessman Approach and wind up as the typical agent who has to struggle and scrape to eke out a bare living.

The trouble with the Average Insurance Agent, is that he's so preoccupied with his own problems and needs, he doesn't take the necessary time and effort to put the next person's problems into proper perspective. This can make all the difference in the world, particularly if that next person happens to be a prospective client. But old A.I.A. can't see six inches beyond that signed application. He keeps running himself up the wall, self-inflicting all kinds of pressures and demands as a result of his quick hit philosophy.

I need. that sale, and I need it now!

This kind of thinking has ruined more sales and salesmen than old age and arthritis combined. I can call a classic example to mind. Jim and I used to do cases together. Since converting to The Blessman Approach, he has found a richer, more peaceful existence. In the old days, though, he was in the habit of eating his nails clear up to the knuckles. I can recall one case in particular that is typical of so many others.

We were sitting in the prospective client's office, the client, Jim, and myself, and the difference between me and Jim was almost a study in caricature. We were chatting away and there I was, easy and cool, to all appearances almost going to sleep. Poor Jim squirmed around in that chair as if it was too hot for him to sit still. He kept throwing urgent glances my way as if to say, "For the love of Pete, sell him! When are you going to sell him?"

Well, I didn't sell him because the guy sold himself as is almost always the case. But Jim was something to see in those days. He had to sit on his hands. He practically ate up cigarettes with the filter and all. Sell, sell, sell! It was the only thing on his mind. And with that the only thing on his mind, he didn't sell very much.

I recall one case in particular. I took Jim along because the client was down his way. The premium was $108,000 on two lives, and I needed Jim's help. Well, every time he went in there with me he almost went out of his mind. Afterwards, when we got back in the car he would ask, "When are you going to ask him to buy something?"

Do you know how long it took for the prospective client to sign? Six months. But that was more than ten years ago and the guy is still with us.

Jim's problem? In those days it was so obvious that it stood in his way. He practically announced to the client, "Hey, give me a break. I need the money. I've got a wife and five kids to support."

Hell, people don't buy because *you* have a need. They buy because *they* have a need.

The Fruits of Patience.

The Swiss philosopher Rousseau might have been writing a sales training manual when he said, "Patience is bitter, but its fruit is sweet."

If patience, as in most cases, isn't an innate characteristic that comes naturally to you, it's one you can develop by generating a constant awareness of its importance and value. I remember that one time a client of mine in Sterling invited me to fly down to Oklahoma with him on a cattle buying trip. While there we had dinner one evening with a wealthy young man who was a friend of my client and was diversified in cattle, wheat land, manufacturing, and a variety of enterprises.

We got to chewing the fat along with our steaks, and this fellow asked me right out, "What do you do for a living?"

l told him and I could see from his reaction that he was one of those super-suspicious people who believe insurance salesmen should be wiped out along with communism and the plague. When I described my services to him, he let me know right off the bat that he had all the insurance he needed. I smiled as if I couldn't care less and told him fine, but that didn't mean we couldn't be friends.

Well, before that evening was over the young man's attitude had softened considerably. He still didn't need any insurance, he said, but it wouldn't hurt to talk about it. I shrugged. That was okay with me. As we became better acquainted, we became more and more close, and months later after a number of golf dates, get-togethers, and telephone conversations, I suggested that if he was interested in what I might be able to do for him, we could get together in my office in Sterling to visit about our future relationship.

The windup is that the case finally went in at $10 million, with another million placed later on, and I can tell you that despite the young man's exceptional caution and wariness, as so often happens, there was a gaping need there that was simply begging to be filled. And I can tell you something else. However crucial the need, our old friend A.I.A., Mr. Average Insurance Agent, wouldn't have stood a chance at bringing that policy home because of those nervous ants hopping around in his pants.

I can confirm from experience that the fruits of patience in this profession are sweet. When you take the time and care to develop a meaningful relationship with a client, the kind that has a solid base of mutual friendship and trust underlying it, and if you do your homework well so that the value of your contribution becomes apparent, you start an association that is longlasting and profitable for all parties concerned.

I could name you clients I serve, not one or two but dozens of them who, when our association began 12 or 13 years ago, were worth six or seven hundred thousand dollars. And I can remember telling these people at the time that in five years they would be worth over a million and a half, and in ten years they'd be worth over ten million dollars. This was after closely observing and analyzing their activities, taking dry wheat land, for example, and sinking wells to irrigate it, that kind of thing. And that's just the way it happened.

As the value of their business and assets increased, their insurance needs increased with it, so that one year they might add $15,000 of annual premium and a year or two later, $20,000, and so on.

Another thing. Working in close harmony with the kind of clients I'm talking about, becoming their business associate, confidante, and friend, all kinds of opportunities open up to you outside of the insurance field itself. In my own case, I have become involved in a variety of ventures that range from farming, ranching, and cattle feeding to the real estate business, so that in some cases my life insurance clients are my partners as well. The same thing would apply to you if you were out here in farm and cattle country, back east in a manufacturing town, or some place where the main source of income was logging or providing services, or anything else you could name.

Permit the Logic To Grow

Most insurance agents view life insurance as a financial tool provided for the purpose of creating a private estate for the client. Thus the goal of the package sale you hear so much about is to create sufficient financial resources so that in the event of premature death the policyholder's loved ones will be well taken care of.

I don't argue this need. It's the old beaten path, and frankly I think it's been beaten to death. The tack that I take, The Blessman Approach, focuses not on estate creation but on estate conservation. There are only two sources of income: a man's work and his assets. As you continue to work and your business expands, your income-producing assets continue to grow. The more they grow, the more protection they need.

The question so often ignored by the affluent businessman is what will happen to those assets when he dies, prematurely or not. To answer this vital question, one of the most important tools at my disposal is the officially compiled book of estate records, over 11,000 of them nationwide, that I discussed earlier. The book summarizes all of these private estate settlements covering scores of occupations and industries, and spelling out specifically what happened to the owners' assets in the period following death. And I can tell you this book speaks more eloquently than any agent could.

It shows how the estates of such astute businessmen as bankers, lawyers, accountants, and mutual fund managers—professional money men—who were strapped for cash when they died, had to be cannibalized to produce enough cash to cover the estate tax and debt obligation. Case after case is on record and the staggering amount of estate shrinkage simply has to be sobering to any man who has a business and loved ones he cares about. And this isn't Lyle Blessman talking; it's every probate court in the land.

The important thing to remember if you feel The Blessman Approach may be for you is that you don't "make a sale;" you merely pull the facts together and permit the logic to grow and prevail.

I have no patience with the kind of slick tricks, gimmicks, scare strategies, and foot-in-the-door tactics customarily associated with the drummer type of salesman. I abhor the use of these terms. Under my system, you don't outsmart the prospective client; you educate him. You overwhelm him with logic. You don't sell him; he sells himself.

In nine out of ten cases the successful businessman is so busy running his enterprise, he's unsure that the problem exists. You patiently point it out to him, permitting the logic to build. And I can tell you the solutions are on hand for the conscientious and dedicated agent to apply.

I mentioned that young businessman who bought $11 million worth of life insurance. Do you know what he said to me a year after the case was brought home? He was trying to explain the move to himself, and he said, "Do you know something, Lyle, you never did sell me that insurance. You simply put two and two together for me and no matter how I looked at it, it always added up to four. In the end buying that insurance was the only logical solution."

Keep It Simple

Leading the client to the inevitable conclusion that life insurance is the most practical and logical solution to his estate conservation problems is as much an art as a science. As you will discover once you delve into the subject, there are complicated technical aspects to estate conservation from the insurance standpoint, not to mention the legal and accounting ramifications that apply in varying circumstances. A common error Mr. Average Insurance Agent commits is to snow the prospective client with a lot of technical jargon he couldn't be expected to understand and which most agents don't fully understand either. All that accomplishes is to leave the layman embarrassed, uncomfortable, and threatened.

Sure, it's important in formulating long-range financial plans, drawing up documents, and formalizing agreements, to understand the technical aspects, represent them accurately, and qualify yourself to select the options most beneficial to the client. But in communicating the basic problems and solutions to him, the technical points are, and should remain, the hidden part of the iceberg. Introduced prematurely they can only confuse the issue. The trick is to get the message across in language and terms the client can understand and deal with as a businessman.

I've stated this to thousands of agents on platforms from one coast to another. The problem in applying The Blessman Approach lies not in technical sophistication and skill, but in taking the system's complex elements and reducing them to the simplest terms that you can. This is a great deal easier than it may sound. As I said, I've worked long hours into hundreds of nights acquiring technical knowhow and expertise, and I won't say I'm not proud of it. But clients have let me know time and again that what impresses them most isn't how much you know but how much you care. They're impressed when you are your natural self, when you show them genuine interest and respect, when you prove your willingness to go out of your way in their behalf, when you make every member of the family feel worthwhile and important, an integral part of what is happening. I find that once you convince them you care, they take it for granted you will be conscientious and honest enough to put the right kind of technical package together.

In the final reckoning, successful life insurance business—or any other kind of business—consists essentially of conducting yourself like a decent human being.

When you put it together from that standpoint it all falls into place. The logic is so simple and clear no technical slight of hand is required. Work generates income. Assets generate income. When a person dies, his working income dies with him and only the assets remain. Given the choices of how to preserve and make the most of those assets, the inevitable answer as I have shown with the use of simple arithmetic is a life insurance program designed for this purpose. Lyle Blessman doesn't have to say this. The figures speak for themselves. The estates record book speaks for itself. And the Internal Revenue Service confirms it in writing.

How logically do the blocks fall into place?

I've done scores of cases in the past 17 years and have experienced only three turndowns. And in two of these three cases I was the one responsible for the rejection because the clients weren't my kind of people.

I have two others who haven't bought life insurance as yet. They followed our recommendations regarding their wills, agreements of incorporation, and other things we advised them to do. They allowed us to coordinate their financial affairs. But they still haven't bought.

So what? Does that mean my time investment was wasted? Not a bit. They're my friends, and you don't *waste* time on a friend. Will they buy in the future? In all likelihood if, yes, the general pattern holds true—if they're lucky enough to still be alive and healthy when the time comes to do it.

That's where patience enters into the picture.

Getting Started

The idea as I said is to run all of the bases, touching first, second, and third on your way to home plate. Before you can get halfway to first you must win the prospective client's confidence, trust, and goodwill. It's another point that cannot be made too often.

Once you win a man's confidence all the rest is just polish. Keep one fact in mind: For you to do an outstanding job for the client you will require information from him that he wouldn't give to his neighbor, best friend, and maybe even his closest relative as well. In short, you're asking this guy to accept you as his alter ego, to have implicit faith in your honor and integrity to have his best interests at heart, and to respect the very private and personal facts of his life as if you were his attorney or priest.

I've been asked, "Do you make a flat statement of that?"

I most certainly do, and at the very beginning. We'll be chatting together, the prospective client and myself, and he may say, "Hey, I've wondered about these things for a long time, but I never had any idea about how to proceed, so I kept putting off action."

One reason people tend to put off action of this kind is because they're reticent to reveal their true selves to others, to bare their innermost aspirations, ambitions, and plans. Family frictions may exist and they're understandably reluctant to talk about them. Marital disagreements may cast a cloud on the picture. There may be conflicts between one son and another, or between a son and the father. These may all bear on the overall financial plan.

"Look," I say, "I don't want you to tell me a thing unless you feel you have absolute confidence in me, unless you're completely certain I'm the kind of guy you can trust beyond any shadow of a doubt. Here are the names and addresses of the people I work with, my at-

torneys and accountants. Here are the other clients I
serve. Here are business and personal references. Before
you tell me anything or make any decision, if you feel
any hesitancy at all, I would like you to talk with these
people, clear up any doubts that might exist. Because I
can't represent you properly unless you open up completely with me, until you share your innermost
thoughts.

"Once we start working together," I add, "I don't
want to find any hidden objectives or facts that could
alter our thinking and planning. I need to have the whole
story. When we open up and go in there to operate, I
don't want any exploratory surgery to get in the way."

Once I have succeeded in gaining their confidence,
they talk about everything; there are no inhibitions or
barriers. Then, if and when the subject of life insurance
comes up, I can demonstrate its value to them. It
becomes automatic. There's never any argument about
whether they should do it or not because we've gone
through all the weighing and evaluating before it gets to
that point. I've gone to the extent of working two years
with a person or a family or a business—two years of
evaluating and studying their situation, incorporating
their family so we can give away stock, setting up the
gift program before any insurance was sold. I take the
position that I am willing to spend my time and talents,
whatever they may be, to the client's best interest to accomplish his objectives.

I'm willing to risk that; it's a part of our verbal
agreement. I don't care when the business is written or if
it ever gets written. I'm willing to risk that with the
understanding that when and if there's any product,
whenever it is, I'll have the opportunity to write it, and
I've never had a man or a business not accept that arrangement and honor it. I've never done the work, no

matter how much time has elapsed, without writing the business when the time came. I'm more interested in a man's confidence than his checkbook because as long as I've got his confidence, the other will follow. You can have his checkbook today, and if you lose his confidence, you're through. It's because of this that virtually all of my business in the past 12 or 14 years has been based on referrals.

Case In Point. I talked about the long nights and days I spent studying, the pride I can take in my business, the rewards I've gained as a result of my accomplishments. Maybe I'm not the most modest guy in the world, but I'd like to demonstrate live how I feel about my clients and how they feel about me. To do this I can think of no better example than Maynard Sonnenberg, the cattleman I mentioned in the last chapter who I helped out in the flood. Maynard is the kind of friend Joseph Addison must have been thinking about when he wrote that "friendship improves happiness, and abates misery, by doubling our joy, and dividing our grief."

Rather than get carried away to the point where I become either maudlin or too peacock-proud, it might be a better idea to excerpt part of an interview conducted a few months ago between Maynard and a newsman who was writing me up for a magazine.

Newsman: When you first began working with Lyle Blessman, what was your reaction to his basic approach, what things stood out that made him seem like the kind of a guy you might like to do business with?

Maynard: Well, the first time he called on us, he laid out the program in a way I'd never seen before. I told my brother, let's bring that guy in here; he's young and he's hungry.

Newsman: How long had Lyle been in Sterling at the time?

Maynard: Maybe a year or so.

Newsman: What you were doing was comparing approaches.

Maynard: Sure, we just gave him a chance. We never had an insurance man do anything other than try to sell us insurance. His approach was totally different. He was nosy as hell, wanted to see our financial statements, know about our business and the affairs of our family. We were pretty close-mouthed at the time so he made some educated guesses, and most of them were pretty much in the ballpark. It didn't take long for us to eliminate his competitors. We saw that he had done his homework and knew pretty much what he was talking about.

Newsman: For reasons . . . .

Maynard: Because he had visited with us and seen our operations, gave some thought to our problems, and being an old farm kid himself, he knew what cattle were worth and could draw some logical conclusions.

Newsman: Did he bring out things you weren't aware of yourself?

Maynard: That's right. Here's what you're worth; here's what you have; here's what you need. His approach was a shocker at first. Then it got you to thinking. He made you realize his conclusions made sense, that it couldn't be otherwise. One of the things that impressed us: He dug out that estate settlement book. I had no more knowledge of that than of the man in the moon. It was a real revelation.

Newsman: Did you trust him at that point?

Maynard: Oh no, not yet, not by a long shot. So I got

him over to the house one night, and in the meantime I had been talking with one of his competitors. And Lyle told us what we needed and proved it by going to the courthouse, for example, and pulling out estate records of people we knew. Well, it hits pretty close to home when you see that kind of thing.

Newsman: Wasn't there another kind of test...?

Maynard: Oh yeah, it's important to know about people, that when they're outside of your office they won't repeat tales out of school. So I threw some leading questions at him; I don't even remember what they were. Oh, I asked as an example about one of our major competitors whom he represented, and he clammed up in a hurry. 'I'm sorry,' he said, 'I can't talk about that.' Back then that business was important to him. He was trying to start a family and needed every cent he could get. He was hungry, but he wasn't that hungry. If getting the business meant betraying a confidence, he didn't want the business.

Newsman: Did you test him in other ways too?

Maynard: Oh yes. I tested his friendship and loyalty. I'd call him at the most ungodly hours and under the most ungodly circumstances. He's never failed to jump when his help was needed. He once told me if there's ever anything he could do whether personal or business to promote our best interests, it would be top priority with him. And he's proved it time and again. Well, you know about the flood on Father's Day of 1965. He got down here almost before I hung up the phone.

Putting It Together

Well, Maynard's very special, of course. But that's the kind of relationship I strive to establish with every client I serve. I hope you get the idea.

"To be conscious that you are ignorant of the facts," Benjamin Disraeli once said, "is a great step to knowledge."

More often than not, ignorance of facts simply means ignorance of their existence. It is why many insurance agents fail. It is why many affluent businessmen's estates are overburdened with debt at the time of their death.

I think I learned a great deal since those early days Maynard was talking about. But even then while I was experimenting and gingerly trying out The Blessman Approach, I recognized the importance of putting it all together by getting as many hard facts as I could. But I tried to get them too fast. I didn't realize as fully as I do today the importance of first winning the prospective client's total confidence and trust before trying to conduct a depth probe. However, once that confidence and trust are established, the next major step is to bring together the information you will need to do the best planning and presentation job possible.

The reasoning behind this is simple. You will have to get certain points across to the client, present certain realities for his consideration for the logic to fall neatly and irrefutably into place. So just as a good auditor or systems analyst would strive to do, your job is to gather as much pertinent information as you can. In large measure your information gathering task will be an accumulation of documents, some of which may date back several years. These will include, for example:

* Financial statements for several years.

* Tax returns, recent and past.

* Title deeds.

* Wills.

* Trust agreements.

* Corporate agreements.

* Partnership agreements.

* Stock agreements.

* Outside investments.

* Origin of assets.

* Joint tenancy agreements.

* Documents relating to gifts.

* Personal, business, and family bank accounts.

* Life insurance policies on client and family.

* Stocks and bonds.

* Other holdings, domestic or foreign.

* Documents relating to ownership of jewelry and other assets.

* Existing debt obligations, personal and business.

* Beneficiary agreements.

You will need these and any other documents that would be helpful in evaluating the client's financial status and worth. It is the kind of estate planning information the client's lawyer, accountant, and coordinator would need to do a proper and thorough job. My job is to pull all the data together and coordinate activities to keep the case moving ahead. After copying the documents, they are returned to the client.

How will this material be used? We will study and assess the various items, make notations in the margins, determine their proper place in the scheme of things. We will want to go back and look at the client's past financial statements and tax returns only so that we can tell what kind of growth pattern he's in, what kind of appreciation to expect. We want to know his assets—liabilities ratio, the amount of borrowed capital he has, about his long and short-term credit history. Perhaps we can improve his cash flow position by transferring some short-term money over to long-term credit by permitting real estate to carry its own indebtedness.

We are interested in knowing if the client has outside investments where a contingent liability exists so that in the event of his incapacitation or the death of a partner or large stockholder a big liability would be incurred. We want to know how his assets are costed. What was the value of his farm, ranch, or other property when he bought it? The attorney and accountant will need this information so that when transfers are made, even if an incorporation agreement is drawn up, assets can be appraised accurately so that a tax-free exchange can be made. Nor can we make gifts to children or other family members to cut down the estate's value unless we know and the accountant knows on what basis cost has been figured.

In addition, we will want to make sure that beneficiary and ownership arrangements are proper, that the way they are drawn up will result in no adverse tax consequences. We will have to determine the origin of property and funds, how much was accumulated after the marriage, how much is in the client's name, how much in his wife's in order to decide what can be included in the client's estate and what can be included in his wife's estate.

Some of the aims and objectives of the fact gathering task are described under "Suggestions and Recommendations." (See Appendix, Exhibit III.) Finally, the client's cash, real estate, facilities and equipment, securities, life insurance, outside investments, other assets, along with a rundown of long and short-term liabilities and indebtedness are summarized on one sheet. (See Appendix, "Asset Inventory," Exhibit II.)

As we discussed earlier, we will also need a whole lot of information that isn't spelled out in documents. We will be asking the client questions no one ever asked him before relating to his and his family's hopes, desires, and ambitions. Often, at this information gathering stage, certain issues may be unresolved in the client's mind. He may not know for sure, as an example, how his wife might feel about perpetuating the business once he is gone. He may have taken certain things for granted regarding his sons, daughters, in-laws, and other relatives. Well, now is the time to find out the truth so that practical and realistic long and short-range plans can be made.

There are things we will need to know that no other agent ever before thought to determine. What does he think of his wife? Personal? You're darned right! You couldn't get much more personal than that, which is why absolute confidence and trust are so essential. What does he think of his children? What does he want to do with his assets and property and what ideas does he have for disposing of them?

The main objective is to accomplish not what you think ought to be done, but what the client *wants* to have done. Your job then is to carry out his wishes with the greatest possible economy and tax savings. Tax economies are important, but they are secondary to the client's desires. That's the basic premise on which we operate.

You ask all these intensely personal questions about his family life with this objective in mind: What does he want to do with the business? Who does he want to be in it? What does he want for this son or that daughter?

Who does he want excluded? What about his wife? Is she capable and competent? Does she need help in financial matters? What bank would be right as trustee to assist her? Who would serve as guardian if minor children are involved?

This is what it's all about. The questioning itself is information. I use a simple blank yellow legal pad to jot down information, avoiding complicated forms which tend to confuse and intimidate people. But I know the facts I am after. And I know the goal that I seek to achieve with the help of other experts involved whose efforts I simply integrate and coordinate.

In the end, we wind up with a summary that pinpoints the amount of cash the client will require for his estate to be settled (see Appendix, Exhibit IV), and how life insurance figures into the picture. (See Appendix, Exhibit V.)

7.

STEPS TO SUCCESS —
PART IV

Throughout this book I keep stressing the agent's role of coordinator as a major part of The Blessman Approach.

That sounds fine, you may be thinking, very neat and pat. But why should a group of professionals like the client's attorney, banker, and accountant—not to mention the client himself—accept you, the insurance man, in this role? Good question. Unless we can come up first, with some good reasons why a coordinator is necessary and, second, with some good reasons why *you and I* should be filling this role, our chance of success will be slim. Well, the good reasons are there in abundance.

The Agent's Natural Niche As Coordinator

The Need for Here-and-Now Action. That the client needs financial management and estate planning assistance is clear. What is more, he needs follow-up action today. Each day his assets go unprotected is another day of financial Russian Roulette. It's like driving to and from work daily on the Los Angeles Freeway without automobile liability insurance.

Wherever you may live or work, I'm sure you see those hearses running up and down the streets at fairly frequent intervals. Well, I can tell you that they're not out there practicing. Most of them are transporting bodies, and one of them could just be your client.

The applicable laws in estate planning are complex, and there are few simple solutions. It takes time to study the individual problems and to work up the answers. A variety of forms must be filled out and documents prepared to convert an estate plan from a proposal to action.

Aside from undertakers and the mayor of New York City, lawyers are the busiest men I know. However honorable their intentions may be, they are often unable to keep up with the workload. I have seen cases where the fact gathering process, document preparation, final contracts and agreements, life insurance policies, and other arrangements tied into the estate planning function are delayed year after year. In the meantime the hearses continue to run.

The delays and postponements are fine for the criminal lawyer who is trying to keep his client from death row, but they are unfortunate where the estate planning client is involved. Clearly someone is needed to hotfoot the proceedings, to get the attorney to act on that case that has been sitting on his desk for a year and a half. And that someone is you. Moving the cases along is an important part of the coordinator's job.

The "Moving Performance." Moving the cases along requires a good deal more than prodding the client, his attorney, or accountant. It's a matter of the coordinating agent himself playing a diplomatic but firm activist role. The diplomacy works from both ends. On the one hand, I'm primarily concerned about getting the job done for the client. On the other hand, I function as a friend of the lawyer; I'm helping him to keep his client satisfied.

The other day I called on an attorney who had been sitting on a case for more than a year. He showed me his backlog. He told me how busy he was. "Sure," I said, "I can understand your position and sympathize with it. But the client is getting uneasy. He wants to see the case closed. There's no point in making him dissatisfied. Can you move this case up to the top? Can you have these documents ready by the first of October?"

He winced. "Let me see what I can do." He looked gloomy and doubtful.

The same day I called on the client. "Listen," I told him, "that attorney of yours is from one of the best law firms in this business. He's the right man to handle your affairs. But I don't have to tell you how busy he is. My advice is to wait a little bit longer. He can have the documents ready by the first of November."

I called the attorney back. "Hey Charlie, I just talked with the client and I got you a little more time. He agreed to wait till the first of November."

"Well, hey thanks," he replied. "I appreciate your being out there absorbing the client's dissatisfaction."

"No dissatisfaction," I said, "I just explained how busy you are."

In the meantime the case was moving ahead instead of continuing to hang fire for several more months.

Another thing you need early in the fact finding process is the medical. It's as important to establish insurability as it is to get financial data. We never take an application until the medical is in our hands. And we don't simply ask the client to take one. We make all the arrangements, set up the doctor's appointment, pick up the client and transport him, bring him back to our office with the medical in hand.

As often as not, it's the same thing with his wife, because if she predeceases him, the ball game changes considerably. At the client's subsequent death, the marital deduction no longer exists. Taxes will be higher in most cases—more than doubled—the need for cash greater, the income-producing assets reduced, so that provisions must be made for this contingency as well. In any case, once the medicals are in hand, we can sit down with the client and talk about the application.

We never send in a non-prepaid application. It's always prepaid by some method. I've had three death claims before policies were ever issued. That has taught me never to take a non-prepaid application. We've done so much work by the time we get to that point we know that the client will be ours. We know he's going to buy life insurance if he can qualify. So why not put the company on the risk the minute you find out he's insurable?

But if you don't do all this work and don't take steps to keep the case moving, no one will do it for you.

Keeping the Total Picture in Focus. Because the attorney and accountant are so busy with drawing up documents, giving tax counsel, and preparing financial statements and audits, they rarely have the time or inclination to look beyond their own spheres of operation, therefore they never look at the client's whole financial picture. Nor do they have time or take the time to explore the client's personal aspirations and desires in depth.

An important part of my job as coordinator is, with the total picture in mind, to make sure all the facts are assembled. I can then say, "All right, Mr. Attorney, here's the information you need to do your part of the job." And I can tell the accountant that the facts he will require to offer his needed counsel are all ready and waiting.

At no time do I try to play the role of the master-mind I let the attorney mind the law; I don't put my two cents into the accountant's tax counseling service. I simply bring it all together so that in performing their jobs, the attorney and accountant, and the banker, where required, will direct their thinking and effort in the client's best interests with the overall picture in mind. It's a task that has to be done, and unless you, the agent, acting as total financial coordinator, step in to run with the ball, no one else will be carrying it or pick it up when it's dropped.

The Agent as Motivator. Although attorneys are now permitted to advertise to varying degrees depending on the statutes of the state in which they practice, most leading law firms are sensitive regarding this subject. Many bend over backwards to avoid the kind of promotion or recommendation which could be construed as solicitation of business. The same is generally true of certified public accounting firms.

The life insurance agent doesn't share this requirement. If he believes an action is in the client's best interests he is free to suggest it and persuade the client to take it. Functioning as coordinator, the agent normally is the member of the team who has motivated or disturbed the client to make contact with other legal and financial advisors with the goal of asset protection, conservation, and proper disposition in mind.

The Agent as Communicator. Too often lawyers place a greater emphasis on trying to impress the client with their sophistication and expertise than on attempting to spell out for him in clear and understandable terms what needs to be done. Here too the agent-coordinator who devotes his efforts to decomplicating and simplifying a sometimes difficult subject, can perform a special and valuable service.

The idea is to enlighten the client, not confuse him more than he already is. The businessman who doesn't understand what you are saying can't appreciate what you're trying to do for him however beneficial that action may be. Nor is he likely to follow your counsel. It's that simple. And after confusing him, asking "Do you understand, John?," won't do the trick either. Many people are reluctant to admit not understanding; they're not made that way. I have had more than one client tell me, "I thought I understood what he was saying when he explained it to me, but when I got home I realized I didn't know what he was talking about."

The smart agent should make communication flow as smoothly as he does the estate planning process itself.

Making the Process More Palatable. I have seen scores of young agents in their twenties and early thirties who are genuinely frightened at the prospect of approaching a wealthy and successful man in his late fifties and sixties and talking business with him. The fear, while understandable, is totally unfounded, especially in this area of estate planning. Very often the life insurance agent can perform valuable service that might otherwise be omitted.

In my experience I have noted that a common failing among attorneys is that they don't like to do estate planning. They find it boring, for one thing, time-consuming for another, a low fee activity for a third. Revenue of two or three thousand dollars for the preparation of wills and trust agreements on a million dollar estate is usually small change to the lawyer. In his role of coordinator, the agent can on the one hand underline the importance of total financial management and estate planning *for the attorney's benefit* and on the other, heighten the client's concern regarding asset protection which will in turn increase the attorney's personal stake in doing the job. A successful client needs an attorney regularly in the conduct of his business while he is living, therefore a satisfied fee-paying client.

Stressing the Long Range Approach. Most businessmen I have seen, if they have wills at all, have wills which are long since outdated. They have trust agreements and other documents, too, which should have been revised and updated years ago. In short, their financial affairs are being handled in piecemeal fashion using scotch tape and a glue pot.

As has been emphasized, The Blessman Approach is entirely contrary to the piecemeal approach. A key objective of my system is full integration and continuing lifelong service for the client, his business, and family. This is in the client's best interests, of course, since it fulfills his needs on an ongoing basis and in response to changing circumstances and requirements. But it is in the attorney's and accountant's best interests as well, since continuing service generates continuing business.

The insurance agent is in an excellent position to think and act in terms of continuing service, review, and assessment. The Blessman Approach avoids the commonly encountered pitfall of preparing a will, trust document, or tax assessment and then forgetting about it. Following through on a regular basis, the client's affairs are reviewed, his documents kept up to date. Experience proves that if the agent coordinator fails to perform this necessary task, in nine cases out of ten, no one else will.

Is the coordinator's role an essential one? You're darned right it is!

A Self-Fulfilling Prophesy

Given the right conditions and circumstances—the successful businessman who has never had a viable estate plan formulated for him and whose financial affairs never have been coordinated with the total picture in mind (and this includes 3 out of every 4 businessmen), and who now takes on a well qualified team of professionals working harmoniously to serve him—I can safely predict that his major requirements, including his life insurance needs, will be satisfied naturally and automatically. It may take time, but the fruition will come to pass.

Needless to say, the quality, caliber, and dedication of the professional team is of the utmost importance to the ultimate goal of providing the maximum in service in the most economical manner. Unfortunately, there are as many underqualified attorneys, accountants, and bankers practicing in the field as there are underqualified insurance agents, and lord knows our industry has its share. In my role as coordinator, I view as one of my prime responsibilities the task of ensuring that every professional who participates as part of the team is not only motivated to act in the client's best interests, but is capable of doing the job he's being paid to fulfill.

As I keep repeating, I'm not a lawyer. I am not an accountant. I don't perform legal work. I don't do financial statements, accounting audits, or offer tax counsel. I step on nobody's toes. I make it very clear right from the outset that I will welcome the opportunity to cooperate with and do my best to assist any qualified professional presently serving the client. I also let the client know that if he is seeking a professional on whom he can place his reliance I will be glad to recommend a legal or accounting firm and arrange to introduce him to a representative. In my practice, I work closely with several of the state's top-rated firms. I also stress to the client the importance of having all members of the team working together to formulate the overall plan.

Interaction is absolutely essential. Attorney, accountant, banker, insurance agent, and client all should be included in the problem-solving and decision-making processes. Typically, a team meeting will run something like this:

ATTORNEY: Will your sons want to step in and continue running the business in the event of your death?

CLIENT: No, they're not interested. Jim is a doctor, and Andy's interested in practicing law.

ATTORNEY: Well then, I think we should consider a buy-sell agreement.

ACCOUNTANT: That makes sense to me. What we'll need is an evaluation formula. We'll need the fair market value of assets.

CLIENT: Yes, I'm working that up with Lyle.

AGENT: What we're talking about is a cash buyout

at death. Fred, what's the estate tax implications of that?

ACCOUNTANT: Taxes normally run from 25-45 percent.

AGENT: In that case . . . .

Do you get the gist of the dialogue? All members working together to put the jigsaw puzzle pieces in place. The agent's role is as essential as the others'. He's the guy who helped assemble the facts, brought the team members together, worked with the client in preparing an asset inventory and other key data. At the right moment—which might be then and there at that meeting or some time six months later—he will step into the picture with the life insurance funding vital to the protection of the client's business and assets.

Functioning in this manner with each professional's knowledge, skill, and experience complementing that of the others, maximum savvy and expertise will be applied in the most efficient and economical way. The life insurance aspect will take care of itself.

The Building Blocks Fit Into Place. As a client of mine says, "It's a natural evolution. One building block goes on top of another until the structure is built."

As each block is added—as the problem is clearly defined, as we place a value on the assets, as we take the tax table and spell out the tax liability at death, as we establish that there's only $7,000 in the checking account—the more clearly the question poses itself: "Hey, where will we get the $250,000 in cash that we need?"

Why should the attorney, a key builder on our construction crew, work with you to put those blocks into place? Because he's a businessman also, because it's good business to cooperate with someone who's helping you, because it's in his client's best interests to cooperate.

I recall one case where the client was referred to me by his bank in Denver. I got into my plane and flew down to his farm where I had lunch with the father and his three sons and we spent a few hours talking. When I came home I had a briefcase filled with financial statements, old wills, and other documents. I worked on these for three or four weeks, then made an appointment to go back there again. This time I suggested that they have their attorney at the meeting.

Well, we sat there for two hours or so while I reviewed my findings and made some rough recommendations I thought it would be worthwhile to consider, one of which was incorporating. It was pretty much a soliloquy. The whole time their attorney, a man of about sixty whom I never met before, just sat there, not saying a word. I had no way of knowing whether he was for or against me. I didn't know whether he was thinking, "Hey there, you young squirt, what the hell are you doing in my back yard? Are you practicing law?"

Well, right then I took a break in my presentation, and I said, "Now, I'd like to hear from your attorney, Mr. Lawmaker."

He looked my way and said, "Thank you, Lyle." Then he turned to the father and said, "I'm going to have to agree with Mr. Blessman. All the things he's recommending are things we should look into and consider. I think we should let him go ahead with what he's doing."

That was my first indication that he was for me, and

at some point I made it my business to make it clear that we would need Mr. Lawmaker's opinion and counsel in exploring some of these options. That's the way it usually works, one professional helping and backing the other, to everybody's advantage including the client's.

Oh, he could have gotten his back up; he certainly could have. But to what avail? He would have been hurting himself.

Not Always Sunshine and Roses. Do the blocks always fit neatly into place, harmoniously, without conflict? Most of the time but not all of the time. There are occasions when you may have to rearrange one or two of the blocks to make them fit properly.

In one case I can recall I was working with Mr. Clifford Turner, a gentleman in his sixties, and some of his people up in Nebraska, and one of the things we sought to do was incorporate the family business. We had proceeded up to a point and I told Clifford, "I think we've gone about as far as we can in discussing this. What we need now is your attorney's opinion, because he's the one who's going to have to draft the documents."

So we set up an appointment to get together at the attorney's office. He turned out to be one of those old time lawyers who keeps the books, does the tax returns, prepares documents. You name it; he's been doing it for years. As I remember it, Mr. and Mrs. Turner and myself were in the reception room waiting to be called, and the attorney, Mr. Crocket, walked into the room to invite us into his office. As I started to follow the others into the office, Mr. Crocket turned to me and said, "I'm sorry, but this will be a private meeting between myself and the clients."

I said to the client, "Is that your wish, Clifford?"

I already had advised him this might happen, and he said, "The reason we're here, Mr. Crocket, is because Mr. Blessman suggested it, and we'd like him in on the meeting."

We walked on in and were seated. Mr. Crocket walked around behind his desk looking somewhat miffed; I could see that the clients were embarrassed. They gave me a look and I sort of grinned back at them reassuringly and gave them a wink. The lawyer settled into his chair and leaned back in it. "All right, young man, just what are your intentions with my client?"

"Well, sir," I replied. "I've been visiting with Mr. and Mrs. Turner over the past six months. We reviewed their financial statements and family situation. We explored their desires and some of the problems they have with the children and with elder members of the family. And the reason I recommended that we meet in your office is because we're at a point where legal advice is required. I've been studying some of the problems, but I'm not an attorney. We require legal guidance and that's why we're here."

That got his ego put together again and his manner softened perceptibly. This encouraged Mrs. Turner to speak up and she said, "Yes, Mr. Crocket, Mr. Blessman has done a great deal of work for us so far, and we're very pleased with what he's doing." Clifford nodded his head in agreement and said, "Yes, that's right."

Suddenly the lawyer was getting the picture and deciding that further opposition wouldn't be in the clients' or his own best interests. Unfortunately there are times, few and far between, when you may have to lay it on the line. Everyone who deals with me knows I will bend over backwards and a bit beyond that to assist and cooperate with attorneys, accountants, and other professionals. But I refuse to let them embarrass me. I've been around too long for that.

The Power of Unique Expertise

If you decide The Blessman Approach is for you, one of your first resolutions will be to distinguish yourself as something more than "just another insurance agent." You will resolve to stand out from the crowd, to become a member of the elite group of specialists in your industry who are recommended, consulted, and referred to when problems dealing with financial management and estate planning—for the two interact and interrelate— develop. Your aim will not be to *sell* life insurance or any other kind of insurance, but to fulfill a recognized client need more knowledgeably and effectively than 98 percent of your competitors will be doing it, so that in the end your product will sell itself automatically.

The philosophy of offering superior service through intense specialization is one that pays off, not only in insurance, but in other professions as well. Law is certainly no exception. I can remember telling a large audience at a meeting of the Colorado Bar Association some time back that:

"Estate planning lawyers are specialists. If you don't see estate planning areas of the law as areas of special training and special law practice—boy, you don't know what's going on . . . . There are different specialty areas of the law which require trial lawyers, oil lawyers, patent lawyers, corporate lawyers, and real estate lawyers. If you have a client with a problem in one of these areas, you would seek help and advice from one of these specialists. And those are only parts or pieces of the *whole* that man works for. His estate is *everything* he works for; everything he does for his family and the wealth he accumulates and keeps depends on the quality of the planning that goes into his estate before his death.

A man never really owns his property; he leases it for only a lifetime, then turns it back, and they call it 'taxes.' "

The typical run-of-the-mill agent is a generalist. The estate planning specialist makes it his business to identify the unique problems and needs he will encounter and tool up intellectually and emotionally to respond to those needs more effectively than at least 98 percent of the agents who will compete with him. With such odds in your favor, how can you miss?

Continuing Education and Research. Another resolution you will make if The Blessman Approach is for you is that you will never stop learning and upgrading your knowledge for as long as you pursue your career. Today's expert will become tomorrow's run-of-the-mill agent if he doesn't make a continuing effort to keep his expertise up to date. Does job security interest you? I know of no greater job security than unexcelled expertise.

At Northwestern, about 19 of us have organized a coast-to-coast study group that has been operating a number of years now. Among us are members with M.B.A.s, legal educations, and financial management backgrounds. One member is a practicing attorney who is one of the nation's leading estate planning experts and who serves as a consultant to two major insurance companies.

We make it a point to meet periodically. The group's purpose is to improve our knowledge, exchange ideas, and keep up to date on the one hand, and on the other share our experience and offer help where it's needed. Getting together from time to time gives us a unique overview of the industry, and of business and economics on a national basis. Instead of having to operate with a limited one-state or five-state perspective, for example, I get a view of the total national picture. I regard the meetings as another tool and strategy that sets me apart from the average agent.

8.

STEPS TO SUCCESS — PART V

A major national problem these days is that too many people are careless about the quality of service they provide. You run into this problem with almost every product you buy, from a home appliance to an automobile. Salesmen work hard to make the sale, but after it's made lose interest in the customer.

Unfortunately, life insurance is no exception. One of the main findings of a two-year study by Georgia State University's Center for Insurance Research, funded by the Million Dollar Round Table, was that too many agents fail to service what they sell. The most significant recommendation coming out of the study was for the life insurance industry to devote more urgent attention to the service function.

"Specific action is necessary," according to the report, because "the total service obligation of the industry is too significant and the sales emphasis built into the current structure is too pronounced to presume that the obligation will be met through natural evolution."

The 1,772 policyowners questioned by the Center cited needs analysis, delivery and explanation of contracts, periodic reports of policy values, and periodic review as services that were most urgently required and too often omitted.

This is precisely what we do for our clients. It's the service they ask for, and it's what we provide.

Treat the Close as a Start

The way I view it, an agent's responsibilities begin in earnest when the policy is placed. Under The Blessman Approach you don't look down the road; you live it on a day-to-day basis. I'm never out of contact with my clients and there's really no limit to the number of people you can service this way with the proper staff support backing you up. All told I have about 650 policyholders with 150 constituting the main body of work and attention. There's a tremendous, but not impossible, amount of work to be done.

We continually review and analyze new financial statements, new values, new markets, increased net worth estimates, buy-sell, corporate, and other agreements in line with current economic forecasts and trends. We update pertinent figures on an annual basis in much the same way a bank line of credit is reviewed at year end, or a balance sheet and income statement are evaluated to determine how much money was made or lost and how the status was altered. Sometimes, after assessing the whole picture, I will see the need for another block of life insurance due to appreciation of values. So in serving the client, I serve my own business as well.

With an operation of this size, to put the picture into proper prespective, I have tailor-made ledger statements run off on Northwestern's computer in Milwaukee. This helps to identify trouble areas and pinpoint specific actions that need to be taken to avoid certain kinds of tax problems. We then update individual coverage where medically qualified, fulfill business and liquidity needs, and so on.

On top of this the review for a particular client sometimes reveals he has grown to a size where his wife should now be included more actively in the estate planning picture from the standpoint of her own life insurance coverage, financial standing, etc. Again, this completely alters the picture and the funding requirements.

Policy Audits. Another vital service my clients ask for and appreciate is that of keeping them informed with regard to the kind and amount of insurance coverage they have, not only with Northwestern but with other companies as well. My people audit all the client's policies. We extract relevant information from the policies the client turns over to us and enter the data on a single audit sheet. Logically organized and arranged, the information is consolidated in one place, so that a balance sheet picture is developed which lets the client know just where he stands, and lets us know as well.

We write letters, sometimes to as many as 18 or more different companies for one client, to get current values that aren't reflected on the policies. This brings us up to date on such information as dividends, premium obligations, paid-up values, and anything else of relevance that pertains to the policy.

Obviously, in servicing a large number of important and affluent clients with complex business problems and needs, and a diversity of holdings and documents, you will need an organization to fulfill these requirements. But that doesn't mean you need a staff at the outset. The beauty of this operation, at least the way I conduct my business, is that you can get it started and moving as an individual agent. You can develop it patiently and gradually into a business you can be proud of and which is as large as you want it to be.

The Payoff—Both Tangible and Intangible. Question the next non-typical and outstanding professional you run into about how he evaluates superior service and the odds are a hundred to one that he will tell you service offers its own reward. You gain from superior service as a businessman and as a human being as well.

Clinton Davidson wrote: "If you want to become the greatest in your field, no matter what it may be, equip yourself to render greater service than anyone else."

And humanitarian Albert Schweitzer once said, "I don't know what your destiny will be, but one thing I know; the only ones among you who will be really happy are those who have sought and found how to serve."

One of the very special joys of our profession is that the life insurance agent is in a uniquely favorable position to provide a service that is needed and valuable. In effect, the message I try to pound home to clients goes something like this:

Let me do for you what no one else has offered to do. Let me be your idea man. Let me lead you through the complex maze of problems and detail, both business and personal. Let me take over your concerns about estate trusts and gifts, buy-sell agreements, valuation formulas, and all the rest.

Turn over to me all your business and corporate documents, long and short term financial problems, and uncertainties. Let me lead you through the maze. Let me work in tandem with your qualified professional advisors and coordinate the ongoing effort to review and evaluate your status in terms of the various tax laws and estate obligations, and in response to changing conditions and growth.

That's the real world today. I know for a certainty that thousands of successful businessmen are out there yearning for someone who is competent, honorable, and sincere to remove this vast burden from their shoulders. If you possess reasonable intelligence and do the job honestly and diligently, I can see no reason why you shouldn't develop into one of the top earners and producers in your area in a relatively short period of time.

Today at last count there are about three quarters of a million people in life insurance sales. Just a little over two percent write a million dollars or more worth of business each year. That means that almost 98 percent are writing less than a million.

The reason they cannot break a million is that they are not serving—*really serving*—the group that really needs service, the group of men and women I've been talking about. One reason they are probably falling short on the service end of the business is that in all likelihood, as the Georgia State study defines it, their emphasis on selling is too pronounced, and their emphasis on serving is not pronounced enough.

Action, Not Advice. Most agents would like to give their clients better service but are bogged down by conventional procedures and strategies which have gone too long unchallenged.

In too many selling situations, in our industry as well as in others, the salesperson has become accustomed to devoting most of his time and effort to "bringing home the order." In recent years, however, increasing numbers of thoughtful and conscientious agents are reaching the conclusion that real service—and real salesmanship—is what takes place *after* the policy is in force. That's when you have to visit the attorney, see that a proper will is drawn, trusts properly drafted and prepared, make sure a proper buy-and-sell is executed, etc. The concept of ongoing service is at the very root of The Blessman Approach.

In our business short-term service doesn't exist. If it does it should be called by some other name. Continuous service, the kind that produces action and movement, is the only service that counts.

It's not enough to do a good job today, present a neatly packaged policy with a pink ribbon tied around it, shove it into a drawer and tell the client with a pleased grin on your face that he's been well taken care of. It doesn't happen that way. A year or three from now, inflation being what it is, and with all of the pending legislation, new tax reforms, the children growing up, the client and his wife getting older, values changing and whatnot, today's pretty package will have to be taken apart, changed, and repacked.

Nothing remains constant. Continual review is essential to determine what your financial status is, whether you have more money or less, whether you owe more or less, whether your business has expanded, added another line, farm, or ranch, taken a partner, added a key employee, whether your family situation and relationships are what they were the last time we looked, whether you've grown to a size where incorporation makes sense, where gifts or transfers of stock are advisable.

It requires continuous thinking and planning. I talk with my clients constantly and spend time with them on both a social and business basis. We bring their audits up to date annually, send them birthday and Christmas cards, take them to lunch, have them to my home for parties, go to their homes for parties. We take our recreation together, enjoy vacations and holidays together. They're our friends; they're an important part of my life.

Many agents will tell a client, "Now that you have the insurance what you should do is see an attorney and get a buy-sell agreement, or get a will, or have a trust drawn up."

They say you should do this or that. We don't say it, we do it. We take him to the attorney. We take the policy in hand and, having already discussed and considered the pros and cons of the matter, we sit down with the client and attorney and have the documents executed. We go over the rough drafts with him, even help him to execute his will, trust agreement, and other documents. We make sure that whatever should be reflected on his financial statement is there, and that his bank understands what we've done so that his credit rating will be upgraded.

We don't leave anything to chance by assuming that the client will take care of it. In our post-sale service we make sure by doing the job literally and physically ourselves. We make the assumption that if we don't do it ourselves, it will never get done. Using this approach, the policyholder learns very fast that we want to have him for a client for the next 25 or 30 years.

The life insurance policies he and his family and associates buy from us are the only way we get paid. But we feel that we earn every dime that we get.

One Hand Washing the Other

Abraham Lincoln once said that the better part of one's life consists of one's friendships.

It's so true. Call to mind one of your really close friends. If you knew there was something you could do that would benefit him, would you hesitate doing it? If you could make his life easier, richer, or more pleasant in some way, wouldn't you welcome the opportunity?

Now take this same very close friend. If you could do something for him that would benefit, not only him, but another close friend as well, wouldn't you jump at the chance? Hey, if you're at all like the clients and associates I work with and serve, you won't even have to think to come up with your answer.

Well, that's how things are using The Blessman Approach. My clients aren't simply my clients, they're my very close and dear friends, and I wouldn't let an opportunity pass by if I could serve them or help them. I've said time and again that I'm not in this profession solely for the dollars it brings. The joy and satisfaction of helping people and giving superior service is far more important to me. But I'm no hypocrite either. As a businessman I'm in business to make profits and enjoy the benefits a profitable enterprise yields. So I'll be completely pragmatic.

The most wonderful thing about this system I

developed is that in practicing friendship, loyalty, and love of your fellow man you are applying the highest standards of good business as well. I already said that my clients are my very close friends. Well, that's only half of it. I'm *their* very close friend as well. When Maynard Sonnenberg as an example, one of my very best friends and clients, is out playing golf with a doctor, automobile dealer, or business associate who is another of his very close friends, it's only natural for him to say, "By the way, John, have you met Lyle Blessman as yet? I've been doing business with him for fourteen years now. Here's what he does for me, and I'm wondering if he couldn't be doing the same things for you."

So he'll set up an appointment for the three of us to dine together, and at that point I take over. I know that Maynard honestly and earnestly feels that in bringing the two of us together he is giving *two* friends a boost, friends that would give him a boost any time the opportunity arises. And that's how it works in this business.

Also, I know Maynard and scores of other clients like Maynard well enough, so that if he fails to bring up the matter, I can bring it up for him. I might say, "Hey, what about this guy John that we ran into the other day? What does he do? Where does he live? What business is he in? Is he the kind of guy that might have the same kind of problems you have? Knowing the kind of service I perform, do you think he might be able to use that kind of service?"

And Maynard is likely to say, "Well, now, I wouldn't be a bit surprised if John isn't your kind of guy."

"In that case," I'd reply, "I'd like to know more about him."

And we take it from there.

Don't misunderstand me. The one thing I make it a
point not to do is put the client or anyone else on a spot.
I don't want Maynard to *recommend* me to John. I don't
want him to go on record as having to tell John or anyone else that I'll solve his problems for him, or do this or
that for him. That's trite and in bad taste, and it lays an
extra dimension of responsibility on Maynard.

All I want is some general information, and I'd like
the prospective client, if he is a prospective client, to
know that Maynard and I are good friends, that we do
business together, and that he thinks highly of me.
That's all the referral I need. It's a matter of using his
friendship to advantage without taking advantage of his
friendship.

So the first thing I do is to make contact with John.
And if he likes what I'm doing, and if I like what I see,
we may get together again. As often as not the prospective client will extend an invitation to me to look his
operation over and maybe do a little exploratory work
for him, and we'll establish a relationship. Later on after
maybe a month or two pass by, I'll get back to Maynad
and say, "Hey, I saw John in Salt Lake City the other
day, and he's got a fine operation just like you said. He's
doing one hell of a job."

And maybe the next day John will call Maynard and
say, "Listen, this guy Blessman was out here the other
day, and he seemed a little bit unreal. Does he really do
all those things he says he does?"

And Maynard will say, "Sure. Lyle has represented
my family since 1962, and he's done a super job. The wife
and I couldn't be more pleased."

Hell, can you imagine how much wear and tear this
can eliminate?

You Can't Do It Alone

The reason many people I know don't succeed in life or in business is that they don't understand the power and value of the simple word WE.

I talked about the team of qualified professionals which, integrated and coordinated through the agent's efforts, serves the client superlatively. Well, teamwork isn't confined to this purpose and goal. It works all the way down the line. For the attorney to operate professionally and effectively, he needs a strong home office team behind him. So does the accountant and banker. The life insurance agent who services a large number and diversity of clients is no different. When he starts, he does everything by himself: the research, review and analysis, clerical work, correspondence, forms preparation, and all the rest of it. When he starts to grow, he hires a bookkeeper-Girl Friday part-time or full-time. When he really takes off, he needs an organization behind him.

My whole life has been devoted to designing this process and making it work. And I can't overstate the importance of the way the organization functions together in getting this objective achieved. It's like when a surgeon walks into the operating room. He's got to have the right nurses on hand, the doctor who assists him, the anesthetist, scrub person, orderly, each one doing his job, synchronizing and coordinating the activity so that everything will run smoothly for himself and the patient.

When the job is done right, the results can be gratifying. I can call to mind one client who serves as the perfect example. His operation is worth millions. When I started representing the family we took everything out of the father's name and sold it to the sons on a note, halting the growth. We recently paid off the note, and when the father dies his estate will show about a half million dollars. The rest goes to the sons, their wives, and the grandchildren. We thinned out his interests and gifted stock when it was worth a fraction of its value today, thoroughly protecting and preserving the assets this man has worked so hard and so long to accumulate. The family can't thank me enough, and I can't thank them enough for allowing me to represent them. But all of this doesn't happen by chance. It takes the dedication and competence of a fine group working in harmony to bring it to pass.

I consider myself particularly fortunate in having an exceptional team working for me and with me, people who are qualified, loyal, and dedicated to the hilt. In 1971, I changed all of my bookkeeping and record keeping over to a computer in my C.P.A.'s office. Every 30 days I get a complete print-out of everything—my life insurance and my other business. The computer is programmed to handle the entire works, so that the need for a full-time bookkeeper is eliminated.

At about the same time I had Dave Stobbelaar join my organization as the administrator of the entire operation. Dave had been administrator of the Denver General Agency for the Northwestern Mutual for 14 years which gave him great insight into every facet of managing a life insurance agency. He took over the administration of my office and supervision of my staff which consists of two full-time agents and two secretaries. I pretty much spend my time in the face-to-face job of serving clients and Dave does much of the work-up and analysis for each case. He reviews all policy audits, makes tax computations, and prepares proposals. As soon as I make the presentation and close, Dave completes the applications, arranges for medical examinations, including any special studies required, and follows up to see that they are completed. He works closely with the attorney, accountant, and me in figuring out the wills and trust instruments and getting them properly executed.

He handles a whole lot of the detail work and does it better, and more easily and thoroughly than I could do it myself because it's his full-time responsibility. Dave frees me up for the thing I do best, and that's dealing with people.

9.

AGRI BUSINESS MARKET

The best evidence suggests that U.S. farms are capable of satisfying any foreseeable increase in the world's effective demand for American food up to, and probably much beyond, the mid-1980s.

Bigger Is Better

Farm capital is being used both more intensively —by increasing the amount of capital per farm and per farm worker—and more efficiently—by lowering the ratio of capital to output. In 1960, the average value of production assets—real estate, livestock, and machinery —per farm was about $42,000, but by 1970 it had reached almost $87,000. In recent years, real estate values and livestock assets per farm have more than doubled. The amount of capital used by the typical farm continues to increase as farms are consolidated while capital displaces labor. In addition, the new technology of agriculture depends more and more on capital inputs produced by off-farm sources. As a result, production assets per farm have now reached $116,500, and by the end of the decade, the average farm could employ in the neighborhood of $200,000 in physical capital.

It is estimated that 45% to 50% of all capital assets are located on farms with sales of $40,000 or more; between 75% and 80% of all capital is employed by farms with sales exceeding $20,000. The larger-size farms use capital more effectively than do the smaller ones. Gross cash receipts per dollar of capital asset run, on the average, 30% higher for farms with sales above $40,000 than for farms with sales between $20,000 and $40,000. It seems that there are substantial economies of scale to be achieved by further consolidation of farm units.

Raising Debt as Well as Corn

Although the use of capital has increased sharply since 1940, the equity position of farmers has remained remarkably stable. In 1973, liabilities averaged $26,400 per farm and amounted to about 19% of assets. This ratio of debt to total capitalization is quite low, considering the profitable investment opportunities opening up in the operation of large, specialized commercial farms.

In the past, farmers as a group have tended to pay off their debts too readily from the viewpoint of maximizing their own profitability. But this attitude seems to be changing. Observing the substantially higher debt burdens carried by industrial organizations, the modern farmer seems prepared to use debt a little more freely. As a result, an increasing number of rural banks are being forced to look beyond their own deposit bases in order to meet the demand for farm credit.

On the basis of a capital flow model, it was estimated that between 1965 and 1969, agriculture used approximately $11.5 billion of capital per year. About $4.9 billion of this amount came from debt sources, while the major part, or $6.6 billion per year, came from internally generated cash flows. By the late 1970s, agriculture's demand for capital is expected to average $20 billion per year. Only about $10 billion can come from earnings generated by farm operations. So about $10 billion would have to be provided by credit institutions. It seems, then, that the annual demand for credit will just about double from 1970 to 1980.

Farming currently represents about 3% of the country's gross national product. It is estimated, however, that farming plus supporting industries such as transportation, processing, packaging, manufacturing, wholesaling and retailing—which share in the economic activity generated by farming—account for about one fourth of GNP. Hence, agriculture in its broadest sense is now, and probably will remain, America's largest industry. As the seventies progress, the U.S. farm will become increasingly liberated from the manifold restraints on its almost legendary capacity to produce. By 1980, it is conceivable that agriculture will not only be America's largest industry but also its healthiest.

Recently John O. Todd, of Chicago, one of America's most successful and imaginative insurance agents and a true industry giant, and myself engaged in a taped discussion about the agri business market I serve. In my opinion, the following reproduced conversation, lightly edited, tells the story better than any other means I could devise. Some of the material in this section will be a bit repetitious of what appears earlier in the book. But I am leaving it in deliberately in order to present a more complete picture of this exciting and mushrooming market and my personal experience with it.

John: Lyle, would you like to tell me what first interested you in the life insurance business and in the name of heaven how you happened to come to a strictly agricultural small town like Sterling, Colorado, to get started?

Lyle: Well, John, when I got out of college, Connie and I just got married and we went to Durango, Colorado, where I planned to teach school and coach basketball. That was to be my life's work. After I got down there and four or five months into the business of teaching and coaching, my father-in-law had a coronary at age 49 and passed away. He had life insurance with the Northwestern and at that time, with a new baby on the way, we were a little disenchanted with teaching and its rather bleak and dreary earnings potential. So it was strictly by accident that we looked into the life insurance business. It so happened that my wife was from Sterling originally. After her father died, with the teaching outlook glum, we decided to go into the life insurance business. We had an opportunity to go to Denver or Fort Collins where I had gone to college, or out to Sterling which is an agricultural community. We made a decision to go back to Sterling for the simple reason that I'm an Illinois farmboy originally and I've grown up in that type of community. They just seemed to be my kind of people. In fact a funny thing, John, when Connie and I made the decision to try the life insurance business and leave teaching, the contract had come out for my second year of teaching. I went back to the superintendent of schools and I handed him my contract and he said, "Well, Lyle, you haven't signed this." I said, "Well, I'm not coming back next year." He said, "What are you going to do?" I said, "I'm going to go into the life insurance business. Going to move to Sterling, Colorado." He said, "Well, Lyle, you're making a terrible mistake. You're 23 years old and you've just finished your first year teaching. You'll be getting a pay raise next year and you'll be in the life insurance business 10 years before you make this kind of money."

John: How long did it take you before you got to making that kind of money?

Lyle: Well, John, the first six months in the business I thought the superintendent was right.

John: And then what?

Lyle: After six months in the business at age 23, and 857 calls as a stranger in Sterling operating out of shoe boxes in our home because we couldn't afford an office, it was touch and go for a while. But I had my draw with the company for $300 a month. It was a raise over teaching and I felt good about that. I was making some headway. I had sold only 25 of those 857 calls, John, for a grand total of $154,000 worth of business in force. On an annual basis that comes to a little over $300,000. It was tough in those days, but I still felt a lot better than when I was pulling down $282 per month in that dead-end teaching job.

John: What did you do then to break out of the routine of ordinary sales volume?

Lyle: Well, John, at the end of that six-month period of time, which was January, 1960, I'd been looking around and there were 26 to 30 other agents in Sterling even though it's a small town of 13,000 population. All the other fine companies were represented and I was coming to the conclusion, as I looked around, that every time I called on someone about my own age I found out that 25 of those other agents had been there ahead of me. So I decided that there had to be a better way to sell life insurance because I'd been reading the trade journals and our company magazines. Fellows like yourself, John, and other agents were writing millions of dollars of life insurance and becoming members of the Million Dollar Round Table. I had it in my mind at that time that you fellows had to be doing something different than what I had been doing on those 857 calls. So I called my general agent in Denver and asked him if he would send me some material about business insurance because I didn't know anything about that aspect of the profession. I didn't even understand it at that time.

John: Business insurance that you wanted to tackle in Sterling?

Lyle: Right. Because from what I could see, the other agents in Sterling, who were older than I and had been selling insurance for 10, 20, and 30 years, weren't calling on these people. I thought that somebody needed to call on these people. They have big problems; they have partnerships; they have corporations; they need financing for their businesses. They're dying and their estates have to be settled and, as near as I could understand, there was a need for life insurance. From what little experience I had had up to then, I understood the farmer and rancher's problem, but I didn't really understand how life insurance could solve that problem. So I called my general agent and asked him if he had any material that might help me, and he said, "Well, Lyle, we have a course. It's a three-year course, but that comes later." I said, "Really, I can't wait for that three-year period. I want to go. I want to read this material now."

I talked him into mailing me several chapters involving partnership insurance and insurance for corporations and taxes, and that's how I started studying the business insurance market and how life insurance relates to it. Around that time I also decided that I'd better have some goals and know where I was going. This was during January of 1960, my first calendar year in the business. I did a little scribbling on my pad and I thought I'd better come up with some goals. So I wrote down that I wanted to write $500,000 of life insurance my first calendar year in the business; $750,000 for my second year; $1,000,000 of qualified business in my third year for the Million Dollar Round Table and then become a member of the M.D.R.T. Now those were my three objectives.

John: Did it take you those three years to accomplish it?

Lyle: It worked out just that way. In fact, at the end of the first year, I'd written $580,000 and I made my goal. The second year I wrote $820,000 so I made that goal. The third year I wrote $1,200,000 and qualified for the Round Table and that was the year, as you remember, that we went aboard the Kungsholm to Bermuda. When I got into New York, saw all those big buildings and walked out onto that ship that morning to sail to Bermuda and saw 1,000 of the industry's giants on that boat, I almost thought I had died and gone to heaven. I just couldn't believe that I finally could associate with men like yourself in this business.

John: You were feeling the contagion of success, weren't you?

Lyle: Oh, very much. In fact, it was one of the most exhilarating experiences of my life up to that point. Getting that kind of Round Table exposure for those six days gave me the feeling that anything in this business was possible. I had certainly achieved a major milestone.

John: How did you get your leads? How does anybody get into this market?

Lyle: Back in early 1960 when I started in this area of business insurance and with the older man, remember now I was 24, 25 years old and I didn't know anyone out in this community other than just casual acquaintances. I don't like that telephone sitting on the desk and I don't like to write letters. Instead I'd rather get in my car. It was the only office I had. At that time I was operating out of my car and my home. I'd decide who I was going to see the next day. I'd get into my car the next morning and drive out to a man's place of business—his farm, ranch, machinery business, or whatever it happened to be—and I'd get out of my car and walk up to the guy. He'd be in his place of business or outside working and I'd walk up, all six foot six of me and young as I was, and I'd grab his hand and say, "I'm Lyle Blessman with the Northwestern Mutual. I just came by to meet you. I'd like to see your farm or your feed yard." That's all I'd say and I'd stop. Here this guy would be 45, 55, 65 years old, worth a lot of money, and owning a lot of property. I wanted him to see Lyle Blessman. I wanted him to grab my big hand and shake it. I wanted him to look up to me because at that time I thought I at least had a 50-50 chance of getting his attention.

John: Now I take it from what you're saying here that really what you did was to move now into the concept of life insurance and people's need for life insurance based upon the business interest rather than the personal sale, is that right?

Lyle: Well, that's true. In this agricultural community out here, most of the people own their own businesses and they are mainly family operations. They have great pride of ownership. They've accumulated property over the years and as you know agriculture takes a lot of real estate today and it's a very technical business. It's a very sophisticated business. It isn't like it was 30 years ago. The father and mother have built this business. They bring their sons into the business and it's a family affair. They have tremendous amounts invested in technology, machinery, equipment. It's just a fantastic business today that I think most people aren't aware of.

John: Lyle, let me interrupt you just a minute. You keep talking about farming as a business. You know city fellows like me and, I suppose, the vast majority of the men in the Million Dollar Round Table, don't think of farming as a business. They don't know enough about it, but more than likely they think of it as they did in the old days when the farmer had enough truck to take care of his family and a few pigs, and now you talk about it as a business. I assume you mean that with these huge investments you're talking about that an entirely different breed of people are involved in it.

Lyle: That's true, John. Today I think it's 1½% of the entire population in America feeding the other total population and we've even accepted the responsibility of providing food and fiber for the world. So right here in Northeastern Colorado we have about 38,000 to 40,000 people total. Well, John, that's 125 miles across this area. Now relate that to the fact, if you will, that we have about 400,000 to 450,000 head of cattle a year in Northeastern Colorado that we have out on the ranches' pastures and in the feedlots where we process them to market weight and take them into our own Sterling, Colorado Beef Company and slaughter them. We ship 90% of this beef, John, to the East coast.

Well, you see this involves fantastic amounts of capital. The owners—the ranchers and feeders—who are raising these cattle, have tremendous real estate that they own for grazing purposes and to grow the crops, and vast amounts of feed grain to feed the cattle. They have tremendous investments in elevators, mills, and trucks and tremendous needs for banking and finance. They may have a line of credit that goes to four to six to eight to fifteen million dollars for just a one-family operation. And naturally they're accumulating property.

You have to be big in agriculture today and get larger and more efficient because the cost of doing business is so big to simply survive. So they have tremendous amounts of property accumulated and it's not liquid. Real estate isn't the kind of liquid and marketable security most of your clients would hold, John. Out here when the head of the family dies, he owns substantial amounts of real estate and has big lines of credit at the banks. Not just local banks; we use major city banks as well to finance our capital needs.

The thing to remember, John, is that when this rancher, farmer, or feedlot owner dies, he lived not only in Sterling, Colorado, but in America as well. He has the same Federal Estate Tax bill in Washington. He has the same State Inheritance Tax, the same probate costs, attorney's fees and administration costs. If he is in a partnership or corporation with his brother or some other relative, the same family is involved. The survivor's interest in the business has to be protected. So we need life insurance to fund buy-sell agreements, and stock redemptions, and to fund partnership agreements. So it really doesn't matter whether it's a public corporation or a large manufacturing business in the major cities as you know them, John, or whether it's a business in Sterling, Colorado. They have the same financial needs. They have the same tax obligations that have to be met when the head of the family dies. They have the same needs to provide benefits for employees, deferred compensation and split dollar arrangements.

John: I wonder if it might not be a good idea for you to give me sort of a capsulated version of how you find it most effective to explain the needs for business life insurance to these people, which would apply whether it was an agricultural business or not.

Lyle: Naturally you don't go to a businessman who

has the type of problems I described and just start selling him a policy of insurance as a package sale. I think that's where most of us make our mistake, John. No, it would be quite the reverse. What I was able to do was to introduce myself to these people, not as a life insurance salesman, but as a concerned and interested person. When we sat down to talk, I said, "Look, Mr. Rancher, you own thousands of acres of land here. If something were to happen to you, what provisions have you made for your wife, who would then be your widow, to pay the Federal Estate Tax bill on your ranch land?" He will invariably say, "Well, Lyle, I don't really understand what you're talking about. I know we have taxes and so forth but I have a lot of real estate and I have other assets."

Assuming he's worth $750,000, for example, he would probably say, "Well, Lyle, I don't really need any life insurance. Good heavens, my heirs could pay whatever tax bills are necessary without a problem. My son's in the business with me and could continue to operate it." Then I point out to him, "Well, Mr. Rancher, are you borrowing any money?" He says, "Certainly, we operate on a line of credit at the bank just like every businessman does."

As you can see, John, I still wasn't talking about life insurance as a solution. I was asking him what problems would exist should something happen to him. I would say, "Are you aware that you're going to have a Federal Estate Tax bill to pay against your holdings? Of course, you realize that most agricultural property, other than cattle, are non-liquid assets."

To get this point across to them I subscribe to a service that publishes the probate proceedings of the estates that have been settled all across the country. As you know, that's public information. It's on public record when admitted to probate court. I literally introduce the businessman to this book. I show him the kind of Federal Tax that gets assessed against estates similar to his, how much the probate costs were, and how long the estate usually remains open prior to settlement. I let him see actual pre-probate records as an example of what can be expected to happen in his own situation. I use this book of estates and a Federal 706 form, which the government has prepared, and I tell him this is the last 40-page tax return your estate will ever have to file. I show him the tax tables from which these taxes are computed and he sees that they are going to take approximately a third to 45% or even 70% of what he's worked a lifetime for. As you can see, John, I've got his attention.

John: And so what you can do now, I suppose, is sort of like Ben Feldman says: If IRS came in here tomorrow and wanted 30% of your business in cash, would it be a problem?

Lyle: Well, John, that is just about what happens, and of course my people are very proud people. They've worked hard and they've come up the hard way and they are very proud of what they've accomplished. They want their son, daughter, or son-in-law to carry on the business. They don't want the property to be sold off. That's opposed to their major plan which is to expand, buy more land, get larger and more efficient, so that they can produce more profitably.

Steps to Success in Selling Life Insurance

John: I'd like to have you describe briefly your present business operation. How do you operate today?

Lyle: Well, John, over the last 15 to 16 years that we've been working, we just restricted our work in this area to trying to solve the client's business and financial problems with life insurance and his tax problem by providing liquidity. This is where we spend almost all of our time. Over these years I have developed a rather nice, comfortable office arrangement and have a fine staff of people. I have a very capable administrator, Dave Stobbelaar, who has been in the insurance business 24 years and has run my office for six of them. Prior to joining our firm, he was the administrator of one of Northwestern's large general agencies in Denver. We have two fine intelligent women to assist Dave in the office so that we have established a professional organization the lawyers, accountants, and bankers—and of course, our clients—respect. I can tell you, John, we're going to be here for a while. We are not just passing through.

John: Would I be correct in saying that as you have become increasingly affluent through the sale of very large amounts of life insurance that it has enabled you to establish your own financial identity and thus participate with some of your clients in their business ventures?

Lyle: John, that's true. In fact I've gotten involved in farming, ranching, cattle feeding, and real estate business, and not only are they clients of mine for life insurance, but we're now partners together in other ventures.

John: Lyle, here you are at the age of 42, your company has been a leader several times, you're making records that are unheard of in the industry. Yet I know that you don't spend all your time at your business. You do a lot of community work, you do things that make your community strong. I'd like to have you tell me something about how you leave time for your family and the things that you do and still organize yourself well enough to do this kind of business.

Lyle: Actually I think organization of a man's time, regardless of the business he's in, is most important. It certainly is true in our business—the life insurance business. The old story is that it takes some men a year to do a week's work and other men can do a year's work in a week. Well, that's kind of my philosophy. I think you have to know where you're going and what you're trying to accomplish every day. I'm quite a family man as you know. I have four children and a lovely wife, and I've always wanted to be as successful with my family as I was with my business. Our life is structured around that premise.

Whatever we do in the life insurance business or any other business venture is, aside from my family, built around my family. Connie feels very strong about this, too—that every morning, unless I'm leaving town, we start the morning off with breakfast in our home and it's a family affair. We all gather around the table. We may only be there 15 minutes before the kids run off to school or I go to the office. This normally takes place about 7:30 in the morning and even the little guys are sitting at the table with us. That's where we have a family tie even if it's only for 15 minutes.

Then I'm usually at the office at 8:00 and start my day. I keep a planner-calendar. I have to. I have to keep it so my office staff knows where I am and where I'm supposed to be so I'm not late some place or don't show up when I'm supposed to be at a particular place, or be there when I have a client coming in. I'm a great note writer. I carry a little piece of paper with me all the time or it may even be the back of an envelope. I write down everything I'm going to do the next day on that piece of paper and I'll put it in my shirt pocket, and when I go home at night I lay it on the night stand. The next morning I put it in my pocket again and it is always at hand when I need it. I'll refer to that paper a dozen times during the day. It is my single greatest time organizer.

I usually have three times as many things on that

list than I know I could possibly get done. I arrange them in order of priority and that's how I work them out during the day. I get in the office about 8:00 and I start on one project or another. The hours fly by. In fact, when it's five o'clock and the girls say they're going home, I can't believe it. It seems they had just come in and were sorting the mail, and now they're going home. I just completely lose track of time.

John: I happen to know that your multi-millions have not come on many lives. As a matter of fact you never had as many as 50 lives in a year, have you?

Lyle: John, I have a hard time qualifying for the company's 50 Lives Club.

John: You just recently had a very large amount on one life—multi-millions of dollars. This is the kind of thing that makes it possible for you to concentrate your time and to be reimbursed or paid adequately for that time because you're not just doing more of the same.

Lyle: That's a good point. I decided early in my career that I wanted to get into the advanced under-writing area of selling life insurance. Of course that means that you're working with older and more affluent clients and you're working with bigger problems. These people have big problems and they have big needs for life insurance. If a person with a problem is successful, it means he has the wherewithal to pay for a solution. So I find that it's easier to sell a man a million dollars worth of life insurance or one hundred thousand dollars worth of life insurance today than it was to sell a ten thousand dollar policy back when I started at age 23.

John: Of course that's so.

Lyle: We know that we will have so many people

that we're going to be working with throughout the year's time because in our method of operation we don't make one-call one-interview sales. We may work on an account for six months or even a year before the sale of life insurance takes place.

John: This most recent big case that you've had that runs into multi-millions on one life, how did you find that lead and how do you get close to that sort of thing?

Lyle: Well, John, I was with another client on a business trip and we spent about three days on this trip staying in hotels together while we traveled. One night during dinner with the client and another man who was in partnership with him in certain ventures, the partner asked, "Lyle, what do you do?"

Before I had a chance to reply, my client interrupted. "I'll tell you what he does," and he went on to explain that I'd been working with him about 12 years and was with Northwestern Mutual and in the life insurance business. He also said that, indirectly, I was a director of his company and that I looked after his family affairs as well as his estate and tax needs and suggested that the partner might be wise to get my services also. Of course, he gave me the kind of buildup that doesn't hurt at all and the partner was understandably interested. So he said, "Well, Lyle, just what do you do that's different from what other life insurance people do that makes him so pleased with your services?"

I replied, "Well, we think we have a professional operation where we're not just selling life insurance—that we're totally involved with our people. We establish a client relationship with them. We totally analyze a man's situation. Certainly your attorney drafts your documents and gives you all the legal counsel that you need. That's what he's trained for. An accountant gives you all your tax advice as he's trained to do. I'm not trained to do any of those things. However, we're trained to go in and completely analyze your financial picture, what some of your problems would be should something happen to you, what position your family or business would be in after your death. We look at the whole picture." John, as I was explaining this to him his eyes really lit up. He said, "Well, would you work with my attorney and my accountant?" I said, "Definitely, that's the way we operate. The only way we can do this is to coordinate the work with these people because at some point we're going to get in front of your attorney and your accountant with you to discuss our recommendations." He said, "Well, Lyle, I own quite a bit of life insurance with two other companies. These men never talked of performing these services like that." I said, "Well then, I guess that answers your question. You asked what was different about me and my operation."

John: What type of relationship have you established with lawyers and accountants?

Lyle: Well, John, I learned early. I heard a lot of older agents say, "Boy, every time I get a sale going with a businessman on a tax deal or something, the lawyer or accountant kills it for me. I lose the sale." They regard the attorney as the enemy. I could never accept that as true. So I resolved to treat these other professionals as my friends, and I find that when you treat a man as your friend he becomes friendly.

John: Well, that makes sense to me.

Lyle: The attorneys, accountants, and bankers have been my greatest friends and greatest boosters. We've established a relationship with them not only in Northeastern Colorado but in Denver. Some of the major law firms and national accounting firms in Denver and I have mutual clients today and we have a marvelous relationship.

John: Just one quickie I think you can answer for me. How does the younger man who wishes to get into estate planning acquire the overall business knowledge to do the kind of things that you have been able to do for people? How does he organize his learning schedule and curricula?

Lyle: Well, John, I think before you can talk with a businessman about his problems—his tax problems, his financial problems, his wills, his trusts, his life insurance needs—I think you first have to examine your own personal situation. If you get your personal needs taken care of and get yourself well established, it's a learning process in itself. You are then better equipped to work on other people's problems and relate what you have learned to their needs.

John: But you're not talking about any specific process of organized study or ...

Lyle: John, I'm a great business student. The more I learn about taxes, law, and financial problems the more intrigued I become, and the more qualified I become to help our clients and serve them. Our company, of course, and many other companies as well, have tremendous advanced underwriting departments that have all the knowledge, forms, and documentation to support the advanced underwriter. I've used all our company's material. As I said, it's one of my main sources of information.

John: So this is part of your public relations approach to your fellow professionals, isn't it?

Lyle: Well, yes, I guess you could view it that way. Just look at the scene. Mr. Lawyer's sitting here in his hallowed office. He's saying to himself knowingly or unknowingly, "Look, we're not just dealing with Lyle Blessman, a 27-year-old agent or 42-year-old agent, in

Sterling, Colorado. This young man has a large century old institution behind him. It has a battery of lawyers who make insurance their specialty. I'm going to use that 100-year-old institution. I'm going to take advantage of that knowledge and the forms that they've prepared to facilitate my law practice for the benefit of our mutual client. I think there is great power there that is available for the asking."

A lot of agents I've heard and talked to around the country say, "well, I don't want to use our company's letterhead. I want to be just Joe Agent. I don't need that relationship." Well, John, we're talking about an institution. It is what we represent. Why not muster all that power and strength behind us? After all, John, what we're really doing each and every day is trying to solve our client's problem, not our agent's problem, not our attorney's problem, not the accountant's problem. And if we can get valuable help doing it, why not take full advantage of it?

Common Problems — Common Desires

Pearl S. Buck once said that "the proper conduct of human relationships is the most important lesson of life."

She understood "The Good Earth."

I don't think I could make the point strongly enough that understanding the nature and makeup of the clients you serve is every bit as important as the technical knowhow and persuasive ability you develop. In one part of the country, as in Sterling, Colorado, the concentration may be on agricultural people. Elsewhere it might be manufacturing, heavy industry, auto makers, and steel men. On the west coast it may be movie people. Or fruit growers in Florida.

Whatever the case, each group will have its individual character, style, and personality even though the business problems are common. And since each of us mortals is in some way unique, within each group you will find marked individual differences. So, although such problems as financing and liquidity are common enough, needs and desires are apt to vary among the individuals you serve.

Agri-business people are extremely honest, ethical, hardworking, and sincere. Their word is their bond. Contracts aren't required. If you shake a farmer's hand it's just as binding as his signature. And once you have earned his confidence and trust, he will be behind you all the way. These people are for the most part fiercely proud of what they own and of what they have achieved. The father or grandfather may fervently wish that his son comes into, and one day takes over, the business. How the son feels about it, however, may be another matter entirely. His aspirations may lie elsewhere, in music, medicine, law, or cartooning. So where does he fit into the business and estate planning picture?

What about daughter Dorothy? Should provisions be made to provide for her family when the estate owner is gone? Will grandson Bill who is now 18 eventually come into the business? Will Mom want to continue the business, or sell out and live on what she gets and the interest?

Such questions are as vital to your planning as any other questions you might ask. Getting the answers is an important part of the integrating and coordinating effort. And beyond this, *updating the answers on an ongoing basis* is no less important. The way Mom feels today is not necessarily the way she'll feel next year or five years from today. The same goes for Dad, Dorothy, Bill, and other members of the family.

Keeping all members of the family happy and treating all of the kids fairly and equally—these are unique objectives of prime interest to the agent-coordinator. Can you see how preposterous and unrealistic the formularized, packaged, quick sale approach would be in an environment of this kind where decisions and actions must be specifically tailored and continually updated in terms of individual desires and needs? In such a situation the package salesman wouldn't even be in the running. And this makes The Blessman Approach all the more appealing and exciting.

10.

THERE IS ONLY ONE ROADBLOCK

    The Blessman Approach. Is it all sunshine and roses? Is practicing it as easy as falling off the proverbial log?

    Not by a long shot and I never said that it was. I hope I am making it clear in this book how much hard work and effort must go into acquiring the basic and advanced business and insurance knowledge and expertise you will need, not only to act and sound like an expert, but *to be an expert.* That's only one aspect of it.

Above and beyond the learning requirement, you will have to develop the philosophy of life and of business, if you haven't done so already, that while Number One is important, he is not *all important.* You will have to convince others, and most of all yourself, that if you dedicate your life to serving your clients faithfully, conscientiously, and sincerely, Number One will be taken care of as a byproduct of that service. Adopting this philosophy doesn't come easily to all people. For some it will mean the breaking down of long established theories and concepts.

Nor is that all of it.

Anyone who has ever sold goods, services, or ideas for a living knows all about "sales resistance." Countless books and articles have been written on the subject; innumerable talks and seminars have been given; thousands, perhaps millions, of sales trainees have been primed and prepped in the art of breaking down sales resistance.

I have been asked time and again about sales resistance I encounter in attempting to persuade prospective clients that it will be to their personal advantage and to their family's advantage to do business with Lyle Blessman on the terms I've outlined in this book.

"Hey, Lyle," I've been told, "come on now, buddy, life can't be all that simple. You must run into some stubborn resistance from time to time. What kind of roadblocks and obstacles do you come up against in trying to convince these affluent businessmen on the value and importance of using life insurance to solve their liquidity problem?

Only one kind of resistance, I reply. People don't object to *owning* life insurance. What they object to is *paying for it.*

I'll get into the specifics of this in a minute or two.
But first I want to talk a little bit about the subject of
sales resistance itself. Because, when you boil it all
down, if there was no sales resistance there would be no
worried, harassed, and fearful salesmen who, lacking
self-esteem and self-confidence, freeze up when the time
comes to call on a prospect, or "close a sale," and convince themselves in advance they can't make it. By the
same token, if there was no sales resistance the average
income for the selling profession would be about $5,500 a
year. In fact, it wouldn't even be a profession.

First and foremost, what is sales resistance? Let's
confront it head on. Sales resistance is the prospective
customer's refusal or reluctance to say yes to an offer for
a variety of reasons:

* He doesn't want to part with his hard-earned
  money.

* He's not convinced that he has a problem or need.

* If he is aware of the problem or need, he's not convinced that the product or service being offered
  can solve it for him.

* He harbors negative feelings about the salesman,
  the company he represents, or the product itself.

* He believes he can wait, that he doesn't need the
  product today.

* He's dissatisfied with the treatment or dealings
  he's had in the past with the salesman who is calling on him, and/or other salesmen in the same company or industry.

* He thinks he may be able to use some alternate
  product or service, or get a better deal elsewhere.

* He feels he can't afford the product or service.

* He harbors predeveloped prejudices with regard to

the salesman, his company, his industry, or the product or service he offers.

That pretty much sums up most of the major roadblocks the typical salesman runs up against every working day of the year whether he sells life insurance or elephant guns. And it's what he must overcome if he wishes to call himself successful.

Well, it's another plus for the non-technical, the exceptional agent, to chalk up. Because here in a nutshell is the beauty and joy of the methods and procedures I use. Almost all of the roadblocks are eliminated. Only the first of the selling obstacles listed above apply to The Blessman Approach. Let's consider the other ones right down the line.

Confronting the savvy and successful businessman with the simple facts of the case will be all you need to convince him in a hurry of the liquidity problem and need.

If you spell out the three alternatives to him as I explain in this book, he will soon see that properly owned and arranged life insurance is the only practical solution to his problem.

If you hammer home the message that you are not a hit-and-run salesman and that your intention is to serve the client faithfully and conscientiously on a continuing basis, his feelings about you, the agent, will be positive indeed.

Once you show him the probate cases that are a matter of public record in his own community, he will be quick to realize that he already has delayed action too long.

If you prove to him that you are uniquely different

in your approach, and that it is not packaged selling but tailored to his own special needs, it will help counter any negative feelings about the industry that he may have developed out of his past dealings and experience.

I have never run into a savvy and affluent businessman who has failed to see the simple logic and good business sense of the life insurance alternative as a solution to his liquidity needs. Once you show the prospective client the light he is almost certain to conclude that he can't afford to ignore this alternative.

Thus the only real roadblock facing us is Roadblock Number One, the prospective client's unwillingness to part with his hard-earned money, the belief that he can keep putting off action until some vague time in the future when extra cash becomes available. As I already said, he probably wants the insurance. It's paying for it *now* that he regards as inconvenient and undesirable. Given the usual set of circumstances it's a natural reaction, but the chances are high that if you do your job properly it will be the only obstacle that stands in your way.

The Manana Syndrome

Shakespeare stated the case bluntly enough: "Defer no time; delays have dangerous ends."

If you defer buying the life insurance you need, your own end can be the most dangerous end of all, for your loved ones and family. The businessman who defers arranging for the liquidity his estate will require at the time of his death will cause all kinds of hardship, woe, and financial loss for his heirs.

The reason the busy businessman keeps delaying the action that is required to provide for his liquidity needs is clear and simple enough. He's alive! On top of that, like every other businessman he is working and operating in a credit economy. At almost any time of the year he could come up with a dozen good reasons for borrowing money from the bank, each of them, if not more important than the insurance need, at least in his mind more immediate.

He needs a particular piece of equipment *today*. He needs feed for his cattle *today*. He needs an extension on a building *today*. There's a lot of repair work to be done *today*. He thinks in terms of his business and its immediate needs.

Sure, he's going to die some day and he knows it. Some day his health may decline to the point where he will no longer be eligible for the right kind of life insurance. He knows that, too. But he doesn't think in terms of that unmentionable day some time in the dim and distant future. He thinks in terms of today, of what he needs here and now. He can't put off feeding his cattle. But he can—and usually does—put off providing for the liquidity bind his estate and heirs will be in at the time of his death.

What steps can you, the agent coordinator, take to combat the deadly mañana syndrome? I make it my business to defeat crippling procrastination by prodding immediate action. Here's how.

Clearly, the best time to apply the hotfoot is when you have stirred up the prospective client's concern and awareness. When we get to the proper point in our discussions I say to him, "Mr. Businessman, we're going to need your wills, trust agreements, buy-sell contract, and other documents that are probably in safekeeping in your attorney's office."

With the best of intentions, he replies, "All right, I'll get them."

But I know from experience that after leaving my office there's a good chance he may forget all about his good intentions, or other more pressing chores are apt to get in the way. So I follow up by saying, "Hey, why don't we do it right now and get it out of the way? Why don't you pick up this telephone and give your attorney a call and tell him that we're sitting here together, and here's what we need. Tell him that I'll hop down to his office, pick up the documents, and at the same time let him know what we're doing since, representing you, he'll be interested. That way we'll know that we will be able to get moving on this thing without any further delay."

What I accomplish by this strategy is to convert the client's good intentions into here and now action. I offer to take care of the pesky chores he doesn't like to take care of himself.

I get the point across to him that he's been married for 28 years, and he still hasn't had his will and some of those other things done. Unless we take action today, another 28 years could pass by before getting to them. By that time he could be too late. And I've got the probate records to back up my point.

It's no secret that people are procrastinators by nature, particularly in situations where they aren't subjected to immediate pressure. If a businessman goes overseas or takes a long trip, he may think in terms of a possible accident or misfortune that could result in his death. But normally life insurance, wills, estate planning requirements and that kind of thing hold last place in his mind. These are subjects he associates with old age and dying. They're unpleasant and a little bit scary. So the rationale runs, "I'll get around to it one of these days."

But so often they don't, unless given a prod.

I'm right on hand with the needle. I offer to take the

entire unpleasant burden off the client's shoulders. Mr. Businessman, you go on running your farm or your feedlot or your manufacturing business. I'll take care of those chores. Not only will I take care of them, I'll go a giant step further than that. I'll integrate and coordinate all your financial arrangements so that you won't have your attorney preparing your will, your accountant working on your tax return, your insurance agent setting up your policies, each one independent of the others. I'll set it up so that all financial provisions and documents are drawn together into one framework and within a single time span so that asset values and personal objectives will be consistent and unified, and your right hand will know what your left hand is doing.

The Hole In the Balance Sheet

Artemus Ward once said, "Let us all be happy and live within our means—even if we have to borrow money to do it."

We are a nation of borrowers. We live on credit and run our businesses on credit. This explains why, although we are one of the richest countries on earth, so many businesses and individuals are also cash poor.

Cash is a glaring hole in the balance sheets of thousands of commercial and industrial enterprises. American home owners, professionals, and businessmen have an abundance of assets: property, machinery, automobiles, appliances, materials, and supplies. But the assets are largely nonliquid. Their money is tied up in human and material resources that are working for them. If you're a businessman you don't keep your cash in a bank at five percent, hide it in a cookie jar or under the bed.

The single roadblock you face in attempting to apply

The Blessman Approach, or any other approach, isn't so much the unwillingness to buy life insurance as it is the inconvenience of paying for it.

Overcoming the obstacle sometimes takes a little hardnosed and practical reasoning. I have had prospective clients say to me with a frown on their faces, "Hell, I can't set aside those dollars to pay for that premium. I'm already borrowing plenty to operate my business. What you suggest would mean I'd have to borrow even more money to pay for insurance. I'd have to be out of my mind."

Or thinking quite clearly! When a businessman makes a statement like that, it's a tipoff that he doesn't understand how insurance works or what it can do for him during his lifetime. The problem as you can see is an educational one. Your response? It's simple.

"Let me ask you this, Mr. Businessman. You say you're borrowing money now, and I know there's a darned good reason to explain why you're doing it. When you set up your ranch, or expanded your farm, or opened your factory, you didn't pay cash to do it; you did it on credit. When you bought your home you probably took out a 20 or 25-year mortgage to do it. You probably bought your car and your wife's car on credit as well. I'm sure we'll find credit involved with every significant move that you made from building an inventory to buying up the cattle in your feedlot. And you couldn't run your life or your business in any other way because that's the way things are done. You can't grow without borrowing. Whatever business you're in, credit is the name of the game.

"That's why most people are hard up for cash. It's all tied up in automobiles, inventories, clothes, brick and mortar, household mortgages, vacations, and payroll.

Some of us own a few securities that fluctuate in value, but when you need cash in a hurry it's rarely the best time to sell.

"What's the main point of all this? Simply stated, most of us think nothing of using credit to fulfill any number of desires and needs. And what we so often fail to realize or think about is that life insurance designed to cover your estate's liquidity needs at the time of death is, if you happen to be a successful businessman, an urgent personal and business requirement that stands high up on your real list of priorities.

"Look at it this way, Mr. Businessman. When your wife and heirs are faced with the liquidity need the price will be dear in terms of both money and heartache if it isn't fulfilled. So it makes all the sense in the world for you to rank estate liquidity insurance as one of your most critical needs.

"The following point is no less logical. If you can manage to pay for two or three cars, a substantial home mortgage, vacations, and a host of business expenses, Mr. Businessman, there's no reason why you can't work the insurance premium cost into your budget as well."

(When the prospect is made to understand the importance, value, and byproduct benefits he's going to receive, if he's smart enough to have succeeded in business, he'll be smart enough to take the action that's needed. Or to let you take it for him.)

Rainy Day and Sunny Day Money

"The reasoning is too logical and clear to refute. That hole in the balance sheet is a pitfall thousands of businessmen keep tripping over repeatedly. Liquidity insurance serves to plug up the hole. Let's project five years into the future. Let's say you have been paying $10,000 a year for estate liquidity insurance. That's $50,000. What happens to that money? You're buying protection, of course. But beyond that what many businessmen fail to realize—because they're too busy running their businesses to think about it—is that three-fourths of that money, $37,500, will be sitting there on your financial statement.

"Well, suddenly you decide to buy another hundred acres of land, add a wing to your plant, refurnish your office, or buy a summer home up at the lake. The last thing you want to do at this point is take out another loan at the bank. You've already made this point eloquently. Okay, you don't have to take out that loan. You can borrow the money you need on your policy. It's a low interest loan, and even though you'll be taking the money and using it, the insurance company keeps right on paying the dividend, and the cash value increases, including interest, which is sheltered under the tax laws.

"If the policy has been set up properly, you get to deduct the amount of interest you pay, and you don't have to pay income tax on the dividends, as they are treated as a return of premiums. It's a wash situation with the values offsetting each other, and you pick up percentage points on the tax break.

"What it amounts to is a form of forced saving with a protection and peace of mind bonus thrown in for good measure. So what could be bad about it? Suppose you accumulate an extra hundred thousand dollars or so of cash in your asset inventory over a period of time. Is that bad? How much of a liability is it to have that kind of money on hand if you should suddenly decide you would like to buy a particular stock, invest in a business that looks promising, pay for your son's education, or withstand an unexpected business reversal or slump?

"Have you ever heard of a person being hurt because he had a little extra cash in the kitty?"

(There's another consideration as well. Any good financial analyst will tell you it's a smart idea to establish a sensible balance so far as your business and personal holdings are concerned. And he'll charge you a fee for his advice. Well, I can give you this advice free of charge and you can pass it along to your clients. Maintaining a sensible financial balance pays off and serves as a hedge against inflation. I've got some of my own money in real estate, a little bit in securities, some of it in business investments and other things, and some of it— what I refer to as my "opportunity money"—in my policies. This is the equivalent of cash and I can use it whenever I please and for whatever purpose I choose. It's a good feeling to know it is there. It keeps growing and building each year and regardless of business or economic problems I may encounter, I know it will be there when I need it.)

"So, live or die, you can't lose. Insurance is never going to hurt you. If you live to be 80 or more you'll be thrilled that the main bulk of the money you invested in peace of mind and protection is being returned to you. If you become ill—and that happens to the best of us— you'll thank your favorite constellation that you latched on to that insurance before the illness occurred."

The Real World

There's big money in theory today and you've got a lot of guys spouting it. You've got analysts and philosophers and a varied assortment of experts advising people to do this or do that, telling them that if they go this route they'll get burned and if they go that route they'll be saved.

A wit once said, "Watch your step when dealing with experts. An 'ex' is a has-been, and a 'spurt' is a drip under pressure."

I have no quarrel with experts. Most of them are pretty nice guys and some even know what they're talking about. But if the expert happens to be a theorist who hasn't spent his time out in the real world, his advice may be misleading.

I've run into experts who would probably claim that The Blessman Approach is all wet, that the principle of capital transfer is wrong. They spout theory to prove it is academically unsound, actuarially weak, philosphically wrong. Yet they can't explain away the simple fact that it works.

My firm belief is that, getting out into the real world, any expert who tells you that insurance isn't the answer would soon change his mind and print a retraction when he saw what was happening in Anytown, Anywhere, U.S.A. He would change his tune pretty fast when he went out there and saw how the world works from day to day, saw people dying all over the place, saw about $30 billion in assets—that's right, $30 billion—put on the block every year subject to judgments, forced sales, and liquidations, saw heirs of the deceased forced to sell off property and give up businesses because they don't have the cash to make the death settlements.

I've known experts who will tell you, "Hey, forget about insurance. That isn't the way. Buy stocks and bonds, puts and calls, commodities and whatnots. You can double and triple your money that way."

Or go broke in the process. Or wind up with assets that are worth forty cents on the dollar.

Yes, there *are* other ways. Insurance isn't the only

alternative. But it's the only *sensible* alternative if what you want is protection at a minimal cost and not crap-shooting with the lives of your loved ones who will still be around when the breadwinner is missing.

What about the cost of the protection, peace of mind, and extra cash accumulation I've been talking about? I already mentioned that it comes to about three percent on the dollar, a fraction of the cost of either selling off assets or borrowing money. The documented fact of life is that for the average businessman it's about as much as he spends for cigarettes and booze during the course of his lifetime, and in a good many cases, much less.

And if you're a successful businessman who is fortunate enough to live for 30 years after buying insurance, do you think you would be upset by the idea that maybe if you hadn't used that money for insurance—and that's a pretty strong maybe—you'd be worth four million dollars instead of three? Experience proves otherwise. Experience proves that the assurance that your three million is being protected, and that your business will continue and flourish after you are gone, will delight you no end. And you'll thank me for having persuaded you to put that money aside as so many already have done.

I like to talk about the real world because that's where I spend all of my time. I repeatedly see what happens when the banker with whom my client has been dealing for the past 15 years calls on his wife to express his sympathy over the death of her husband. His feeling is sincere and he sheds an honest tear over dear Bill's departure.

"But you know, Mrs. Client," he adds, "Bill had this note with the bank and it simply has to be paid."

And I've heard Mrs. Client reply, "That's all right, Mr. Banker. You see, I have this $200,000 check from the insurance company to cover all of the taxes, debts, and other expenses."

Well now, let the expert tell Mrs. Client at that point that he knows of some better way. It might be interesting to hear what she answers.

You Have It—You See It

Properly established life insurance, planned for asset protection through ample liquidity when liquidity is needed the most, has proved itself time and again to be one of the most important tools in the businessman's kit. But most people have little appreciation for a tool until they *can see its value* and put it to use. It's like a superbly crafted old violin you have sitting upon a shelf for years. You don't really appreciate its worth until someone takes it down from the shelf, dusts it off, and applies a bow to the masterpiece.

Well, that's another one of the beauties of The Blessman Approach in general and the capital transfer concept in particular. The value is right there on hand for the client to see and appreciate. You can bet your sombrero it is. In fact, your accountant will carry the value right on your books as an asset that will keep building each year.

It's like having your own personal bank with a line of credit that's always open to you.

Yes, sir. For as long as you live you will have a steady influx of cash flowing into that bank via the life insurance premiums that you pay each year. And if you don't take the trouble to check the value of this buildup on your financial statement and books, if your operation is incorporated it will be done for you at the end of each year. In all our corporate situations, a computer cash value printout is produced by Northwestern's home office and it's sent to the client.

So, however you slice the pie, in lean years or prosperous, live or die, the client's heirs and estate are always ahead of the game, and the visibility to prove it is there.

11.

THE WILSON FAMILY

This chapter will be devoted to a case history describing the origin and development of one of our important accounts. The Wilson family referred to is an actual client, one of many such clients. In view of the personal nature of the information divulged and in the interests of client confidentiality, always a prime consideration, the names and type of business of the family members and closely connected associates have been disguised. But the facts of the case are real. The purpose of this chapter is to demonstrate how The Blessman Approach actually works in a live field situation, and to give the sequence of steps as they happen.

The Initial Contact

As I discussed earlier in this book, The Blessman Approach virtually eliminates "cold canvassing" of accounts in the conventional sense. When genuine, continuing service of the kind that was discussed and described occurs, prospective clients seek *you* out on a fairly regular basis or, through your own discreet inquiries via third person intermediaries, become interested in what you have to offer them. In one case a direct client referral will lead to the contact. In another case a referral by an attorney, accountant, or banker will lead to the contact. In a third situation, your interest as the agent might be provoked by a particular businessman or professional, in which case your mention of this interest to a mutual acquaintance or associate will result in his working in your behalf to bring you and the prospective client together.

In the case of the Wilson family, Charley Baldwin, a banker who is aware of our reputation of competence in the life insurance industry and of servicing substantial clients over the years, called us in to discuss a loan customer. The bank had enjoyed a long time relationship with the Wilsons as they had with me and suggested to them that they review their grain farm operation and holdings with estate planning for the father in mind so that the business would pass on to the three sons smoothly, harmoniously, and without undue cost. The farm spread amounted to approximately 6,000 acres, with about $450,000 worth of equipment in grain drill, stack hand, and 4-wheel-drive tractors, combines, swathers, grain box, and pickup trucks.

Charley Baldwin already had informed the father, John Wilson, that a number of the bank's major clients were using the services of the Blessman organization. He suggested to the prospective client that he pay us a visit and have us analyze the situation and recommend what actions we thought ought to be taken. Mr. Wilson thought this sounded like a good idea and phoned our office in Sterling. Arrangements for the initial meeting in Denver were made.

The First Meeting

I met John Wilson, who since has become a close and dear friend, on the pre-arranged date at the bank's conference room in Denver. He had brought his three sons along with him. We were introduced by Charley Baldwin, who is the bank's senior loan officer. Charley gave the Wilsons a brief rundown on the Lyle Blessman organization, and repeated that the reason he had brought us together was because of our history and experience of working with bank customers and the reputation we enjoyed.

I then explained in greater detail who I was, who the members of the Blessman team were, and how we worked. I pointed out that I was in the life insurance business and that life insurance was my sole means of income. I also made it clear that in spite of this, life insurance was simply a byproduct of the total service we performed. I further explained that I had been in the business since 1959 and that, in addition to my staff of four people, I enjoyed a mutually beneficial working relationship with several important and well established law and accounting firms. The names of these firms, some of which are among the nation's largest and most prestigious, were both familiar and impressive to the Wilsons.

One message I made it my business to get across right at the outset was that we were in business, not just to sell life insurance for the sake of the commission involved, but to develop a continuing long-term relationship with the client.

"To achieve this," I explained, "it is important that you develop total confidence in me and in my ability to serve you and fill your needs."

I also let it be known that we were not attorneys or C.P.A.s and, therefore, did not offer tax or legal advice. Our job was to gather the facts, analyze the situation, determine their personal desires and aims, and in order to fill their needs and meet their objectives, coordinate relevant decisions and actions with their other financial advisors.

John Wilson asked, "What will your analysis consist of?"

"It will cover two general areas, " I explained. "First, we will need copies of all your personal and business financial documents. This will include your financial statements and tax returns, business and personal, for the past five years. We will build a fair market asset inventory from the start of your business life. We will need all legal documents pertaining to partnership or corporate interests and agreements; we will need copies of wills, trust documents, gift tax returns, a complete list of all long and short-term liabilities and mortgages along with the terms of repayment. We will need information and documentation to support your own and your wife's individually and jointly owned assets. We will have to have a breakdown of all assets and properties with inheritance potential from both sides of the family. Finally, we will need all life insurance policies, both business and personal.

"The second area of analysis," I explained, "is geared to bring your personal and business desires into proper perspective. In many instances these are not even articulated unless and until such an analysis is made."

I said, "We will have to determine where you, your

sons, and your associates have been in your personal and business careers, where you are now, and what you have in mind for the future."

I told Mr. Wilson and his sons how, after collecting all of this information and getting a clear definition of their desires and objectives, we analyze the overall situation and spell out the financial problems and roadblocks we come up with. We then present the different options and solutions as we see them and recommend what we believe to be the most viable alternatives.

One of the Wilson sons said, "That sounds like a lot of work, Mr. Blessman. You mean to say there's no charge for this service?"

"None whatsoever. This is what you can expect from us, and we're willing to take the responsibility of producing it. We do the analysis work, invest our time, energy, experience, and talent to develop a plan of action which we believe will satisfy your business needs most economically and fulfill your personal objectives in the best possible manner. But we're not running a charitable organization. What we expect in return is that if you put our business and estate planning recommendations into effect, and assuming that you and your other advisors agree that life insurance as a funding vehicle is required as part of the plan, that you will buy the life insurance from us. Obviously, I express that expectation with the full knowledge that for the request to be met our product must be competitively priced."

Mr. Wilson exchanged glances with his three sons and their banker.

"That sounds fair and reasonable to me."

"Keep in mind," I added, "that what we seek is a

long and continuing relationship based on value and trust. It has been my experience that our responsibility and service only *begin* at this initial design and funding stage of your business and personal plans. We feel it is also our responsibility to see the agreed upon plans and actions executed on the one hand, and on the other kept current with the passing of time as regards changes in the tax law and other pertinent legislation as well as your own changing needs and desires. Our aim," I concluded, "is through dedication and service, to earn a respected position on your personal and financial advisory team. If we do our job right, the recommendations we make following the initial analysis will be so well considered and all inclusive that the wisdom of their implementation will be borne out five, ten, and twenty years into the future."

The Wilsons agreed that our approach and the terms of our working relationship made sense and promised to gather all of the documents I had requested and spell out what their personal and business aims and desires were at this time. A date was set for us to pick up the documents preparatory to conducting the analysis. At that point the meeting was adjourned.

The Initial Analysis

Three weeks later my associate, Dave Stobbelaar, who would be responsible for much of the spade work, and myself flew our plane to the airport that is in the general Springfield, Colorado area where the Wilson farm is located. John Wilson met us at the airport and drove us in his Cadillac to the farm's office where all the documents were turned over to us and receipted. We also got the Wilsons' permission to consult with our own financial experts after completing the preliminary phase of our study.

After enjoying lunch with the Wilsons and some of their people, we flew back to our headquarters in Sterling and got to work on the task of studying the financial situation, pinpointing the problems, and making our recommendations to solve them. We then took the documents and our findings to the attorneys, accountants, and home office experts we work with in Denver, and had them review our assessments and the problems we had spelled out. We do this not only to confirm our own findings and judgment, but to add credibility to our analysis.

After this we dropped in on Charley Baldwin, the banker who had made the referral, showed him the financial statements and reviewed past borrowing patterns and projected future credit needs. This entire review and consultation spanned a three-week time period after which I phoned the Wilsons for an appointment to review our findings with them. I suggested it would be a good idea for their own local attorney to be present at this meeting.

Meeting Number Two

At the prearranged time and date, Dave Stobbelaar and myself flew back out to Springfield. The meeting was held in the clients' office with the four principals, their attorney, Dave, and myself. We had prepared copies of the summary for each participant, including Mr. Walker, their attorney. We made the presentation with the aid of an easel and flip chart, representing the facts as we found them:

1. The need to make family transfers of money and other assets by way of gifts.

2. The need to establish estate liquidity in behalf of John Wilson, and to keep enough holdings in his

name to ensure that he and Mrs. Wilson would always be self-sufficient.

3. John Wilson's desire to guarantee that all of the business interests would go to his three sons in the business during their lifetime, and that after his death they would be assured of full ownership and control.

4. The desire that all nonbusiness assets of the mother and father, John and Rose Wilson, would go to their married daughter presently living in Kansas.

5. The need to peg the value of the stock that was in the father's name for estate tax purposes, and to allow future growth of these securities to accrue to his sons and grandchildren according to predetermined apportionment.

6. Problems relating to the three sons' individual estates as a result of their one-third ownership of the family business.

7. The desire for the business to continue after John Wilson's death.

8. The requirement for a buy-sell agreement for the disposal of family business stock so that the farm entity could be perpetuated and so that the heirs could receive the fair market value of the stock in trust in a cash settlement in order to: (a) meet the estate's liquidity needs, and (b) enable the farm to produce continuing income for the heirs.

9. The need to establish key man life insurance for the business to indemnify the owners for the loss of management talent and the corresponding profit dip it would generate. This supports the long proven premise that it is management, not capital, which produces profits. Capital is merely

a commodity that earns a rate of return. Any gain beyond that is ascribable to management expertise and ingenuity.

10. The requirement to make funds available for debt reduction to keep lines of credit in a secure position.

This presentation took two hours. When it was completed, the attorney, Harold Walker, who had served the clients for about seven years, addressed John Wilson and his sons. "Gentlemen, I strongly agree with the situation as presented and the recommendations made by Mr. Blessman and his associate. I suggest that you follow their advice to the letter."

John Wilson nodded. "Where do we go from here?"

I replied, "I would suggest that we all meet in Denver with our attorneys and tax accountants to review the technical, legal, and tax aspects that pertain to the arrangements as outlined. We should also have rough drafts of the documents we will need on hand so that our master plan for the continuation cf the business, the family transfers of assets, and the four individual estate plans can be coordinated."

The objective of this, I explained, was to bring together the four principals, their attorneys, our attorney, accountants, and associates to bring everyone's inputs into the consideration of the problems and proposed solutions. All parties went along with this suggestion.

Meeting Number Three

A week later an all-day meeting was held in Denver. The total master plan was agreed upon with a few minor

changes because of tax considerations and the attorney's need to coordinate the business and personal
documents. We recommended at this session that
everyone get medical examinations as soon as possible
to determine the insurability of the principals because if
any one of the Wilsons was uninsurable, the legal documents would have to be revised because of the lack of
funding. Again all parties agreed.

The Physical Exams

Medical appointments for all four Wilsons were set
up for the following day. Dave Stobbelaar and I spent
that night in a Denver hotel. The next morning we personally transported the clients to Northwestern's ex-
aminers and waited while they were examined. They
were all physically fit and thus qualified for life insurance. After lunch we reconvened and took prepaid applications on the family for seven million six hundred thousand dollars.

Execution of the Plan

The next step was to convert the master plan from
paper to reality. A succession of transactions followed
with this purpose in mind:

* We transferred the allowable maximum amount of
stock from John Wilson's ownership to that of his three
sons, their wives, and their children to the extent of the
specific exemption and annual exclusion which at that
time existed.

* We received the mother's consent allowing the
transferred amount to be doubled. Under this arrangement we could transfer the maximum amount of stock
out of the father's estate.

* The remaining amount of stock that was owned by John Wilson was sold to his three sons and their wives.

* The notes were set up so that John Wilson could use the annual gift exclusion forgoing that portion of the note each year.

* We got the gift mechanisms into the works. The amount of life insurance we placed on the father was sufficient to satisfy the estate's entire liquidity needs from the inception due to the fact that three years would have to pass to assure that the gifts' value would be excluded from the estate. Enough cash was on hand in the remainder of the estate to cover grandfather gifts to his sons' children. We did this to the maximum allowable amount of $6,000 per grandchild per year. We bought substantial amounts of life insurance on each grandchild with the cash gifts. This had the effect of (1) getting the cash out of the grandfather's estate, and (2) getting the insurance in force on the new children stockholders who would have future liquidity needs for their own estates, all of which was accomplished at a very young age and with very low premium requirements.

* At the time of the underwriting we also placed a substantial amount of insurance on each grandchild stockholder, apart from the insurance that had been purchased with the cash gifts. These policies were owned by the corporation and were provided for future key man coverage and as a vehicle for funding the buy-sell to which their stock was restricted.

* In addition, the major block of insurance that we placed on each of the three sons was owned by the corporation as key man insurance to (1) provide liquidity for their individual estates through a Section 303 redemption; (2) fund the stock redemption agreement between the deceased's family and the corporation; and

(3) provide sufficient liquidity to meet anticipated corporate debt and indemnify the corporation against loss of income brought about by the death of a member of the management team.

From the Bank's Perspective

Charley Baldwin, the bank's senior loan officer and his boss, the senior vice president, were completely satisfied with the master plan and its execution. For one thing it assured the bank's officers that if death occurred to John Wilson or any one of his sons, the need for cash generated by the death would not require additional borrowing at a time when a disruption of the business might be expected. They were also convinced that the farm would continue to operate profitably since all debts along with financial and individual lifestyle requirements would be provided for.

Expressing his reaction from the banker's point of view, Charley said, "Instead of a principal's death causing increased demands on credit, it would have just the opposite effect. It would create in the form of tax free life insurance the dollars required to meet the estate's liquidity needs, the cash needed for stock redemption to produce income for the deceased's family on the one hand, and on the other hand bring cash into the corporation's surplus account, not only to indemnify the business against the loss of management profits, but to provide money for debt reduction as well."

Keep in mind that the cost of owning the insurance during their lifetime is relatively inexpensive compared to the alternatives discussed earlier in the book. The premium represents only about half the interest on the total funds required and the main bulk of these premium dollars keep accumulating on the balance sheet as cash reserves in corporation-owned life insurance. This is therefore available to the corporation and its owners as required during the course of their lifetime.

Expanded and Continuing Analysis

We subsequently reviewed the individual estates of the three Wilson sons and determined that if the wives should predecease them, it would cause the sons to lose the marital deduction. We calculated what the value of the marital deduction on each of the wives would be. We then had the wives examined and purchased life insurance to bring cash into the estate in the event of their death to offset the loss of the marital deduction.

The next step was to analyze the business's key employees who were not part of the family and to work up a viable fringe benefit program to retain them and compensate them for their dedication and service. This led us to recommend a deferred compensation contract from the corporation which would provide salary continuation for the employee's family in the event of his premature death. Retirement benefits were also included. We then funded this program with cash value life insurance to make sure that the funds would be there to meet contractual obligations in the event of death or retirement. Five key employees outside the family were involved in these transactions.

Gloria. As values continued to grow along with the continuing growth of the business, John and Rose Wilson wanted to make sure that Gloria, their married daughter who was living in Kansas, received her fair share of the estate. Our recommendation was that the corporation take out additional life insurance in the amount of $500,000 on the father under a split dollar arrangement. The way this works is that the corporation pays the entire premium and owns and controls the policy's cash value. The daughter owns the amount at risk, is named beneficiary, and the insured father accepts the resultant P.S. 58 cost. The end result of this agreement is to bring risk money to the daughter via the policy paid for by the family corporation and owned outside of the father's taxable estate.

Group Insurance. In an advisory capacity we analyzed the group life and hospitalization requirements of all corporate employees. This led to the following actions, reviews, and decisions:

* We designed group insurance specifications to meet the requests of the owners to make adequate provisions in behalf of all employees.

* After ordering and reviewing bids from insurors, we placed the coverage in force to the best advantage of the corporation and its people.

* We reviewed an existing qualified pension plan that was in force at the time. Our determination was that since the plan had been in existence for a number of years, it had become inadequate and somewhat obsolete as a result of the corporation's profitability and growth and the introduction of ERISA in 1974.

* With the Wilsons' approval, we showed the existing pension plan to our attorneys in Denver and recommended that their Qualified Plan Attorney review the arrangement and make recommendations to bring it up to date and provide for ERISA compliance. This entailed a trip to Denver for Dave Stobbelaar and myself, where we spent a half day with our attorneys and their specialist redesigning a combination pension and profit-sharing plan.

* After approximately six months of calculations

and review, the new plan was finalized and adopted.

Long-Term Involvement. During this same period the Wilsons hired Bill Chapman, a practicing attorney who had been serving them over the years on an on-and-off basis, as their financial vice president and corporate in-house counsel. We wholeheartedly endorsed this move in view of the company's rapid growth and growth projections, and the continuously increasing complexity of the business.

We were assigned the responsibility of reviewing all financial planning and implementations over the past ten years with this new executive. As far as I was concerned, this represented an outstanding opportunity to be of service to the client on the one hand, and on the other hand to establish a mutual relationship of confidence and trust with Mr. Chapman. He readily accepted and appreciated our cooperation and assistance. I might add that our coordinated efforts have proved invaluable in accomplishing our shared objective of integrating the client's financial affairs in the most beneficial and economical way.

As far as our relationship and dealings with the client are concerned, we are periodically consulted on business and personal problems that arise from day to day and have come to be regarded as de facto members of the corporate executive team. We assist the accountants each year in their preparation of financial statements by providing annual audits of all life insurance policy values as well as computer printouts of the effect of these policies on corporate cash flow and balance sheet items. Also on an annual basis, we help to determine the value of stock as a means of updating buy-sell agreements and establishing the value of gifts.

From time to time major acquisitions are contemplated by the Wilsons which may or may not be consummated; in such cases as required we assist in finding long-term financing. When employees with specific qualifications are needed, we help in the trackdown of available talent. We have become associate members of the Wilsons' farm and trade organizations, and contribute financially to a number of causes they espouse; in effect and selectivity, of course, their causes become our causes. We are, after all, "part of the family."

We attend the corporation's annual meetings and make every effort to familiarize ourselves with their industry problems and to gain a more complete understanding of the unique aspects of their highly specialized business. We have been tapped on a number of occasions as banquet speakers, or to conduct lectures or seminars for business and estate planning before industry groups in which the Wilsons participate. We set up marketing seminars for the corporation's sales people and freely contribute our particular expertise and experience in an effort to enhance their own sales efforts.

On a more personal note, I have been requested by John and Rose Wilson from time to time to speak privately with their sons and daughter to help clarify their own roles in the family business and their personal aims and desires, business-related and otherwise.

What It All Adds Up To

At this point in the book it's no secret to anyone that the main thrust of The Blessman Approach is unique service in the form of financial consultation, analysis, and the coordination of the client's financial affairs. As you can see from the case history outlined in this chapter, we offer this service on a continuing basis and as part of the corporate family *with no consulting fee charged.* The only compensation we receive is the commission on the life insurance policies we place. In view of the fact that these policies often run into millions of dollars and are continually augmented as funding requirements increase over the years, we believe we are more than adequately paid for the work that we do—not to mention the most important payment of all that is in terms of real lifelong friendship and trust and the joy and satisfaction we derive from the contribution we make.

12.

CONVERT THE BLESS-MAN APPROACH TO THE <u>YOU</u> APPROACH

The most important person in your life is YOU. If you believe in yourself you will become believable to others. They will trust what you say and do. You will be better equipped to help the clients you serve achieve their goals and desires, and in the process you will be helping yourself. If I learned one thing after applying The Blessman Approach over the past 19 years, it is that serving yourself is an automatic byproduct of serving other people. Thus the others come first.

What I tried to demonstrate, describe, and explain in this book is a system that works. Over the years I have been able to prove to my own satisfaction, to my clients' satisfaction, and to the satisfaction of scores of people who have worked with me and for me, that if you take certain actions—become knowledgeable, contact certain prospective clients, think in terms of long-range client gains instead of quick-kill personal gains—success as a life insurance agent will be predestined and inevitable.

The question, of course, is: Will you be able to take The Blessman Approach and adapt it to your own personal use? *I know you can do it because dozens of agents already have done it.* I have personally witnessed them doing it, and I have seen the rewards that they reaped.

If you are reasonably intelligent, not offensive to others, a normal and wholesome looking individual, with basic training as an insurance underwriter and a general knowledge of business, finance, and the tax structures that work in our system, there's no reason I can conjure up that you shouldn't be able to duplicate for yourself the pattern of service and success I developed over the years. Well, perhaps that's not totally accurate. To apply The Blessman Approach, or any other system, effectively, you must first have a burning desire to succeed at it and next, be prepared to invest the time, effort, and work required to qualify yourself to succeed at it. Given these basics, I don't see how you can help but succeed.

All right. At this point let's take a hard back-from-the-trees look at this brainstorm I have been so proudly referring to as The Blessman Approach. Actually, what is it all about? Well, it has been described step-by-step in this book. You've seen it developed and built from its first basic origins. You've seen how it works in real life from the case history example outlined in Chapter

Eleven. But so far, you've seen the Blessman Approach only through the eyes of Lyle Blessman. (Which, I suppose, is only natural, since it was good old Lyle who developed it.) My intentions, though, run a lot deeper than just singing my own praises. My objective is to help *you.*

Your objective, if you now wish to duplicate the success I enjoy, is to convert this system so that it will be The Jones Approach if your name is Jones, The Smith Approach if it's Smith, The Mulligan Approach if your name is Mulligan. In short, to make this plan work you will have to think of it as *your* plan, not the plan of some guy named Blessman who is a thousand miles away. Make it your personal success plan and you will develop confidence and faith in the system. You will imbue it with a pride of love and creation and ownership as I have done with The Blessman Approach. *You will identify with it individually and personally,* an all-important requirement.

How can you convert The Blessman Approach to the Jones, Smith, or Mulligan Approach?

Step One: Adapt the basic ingredients and framework as outlined in this book.

Step Two: Tailor The Blessman Approach to your own specific aims and requirements and to your prospective clients' individual needs. If you are located in horse raising country, for example, become an expert on the raising of horses. If your principal prospects are medical men, learn as much as you can about the doctor's personal, professional, and financial needs. If you plan to call on a whole lot of shipbuilders, study the shipbuilding industry until you become conversant with it.

We live in a specialized age. Become a life underwriting specialist, an estate planning specialist, a financial analyst, a specialist in one or more industries. This will make you stand out in your field. It will separate you from the other 99 agents in your area who are simply peddling policies. Take my word for it, it works. And if it works in Sterling, Colorado, there's no reason on earth that it won't work just as well in Bangor, Maine, Twin Falls, Idaho, New York City, or any place else in this golden land of opportunity.

Step Three: Think of the approach as your personal approach as indeed in time it will be. Don't be afraid to experiment. Keep the system flexible, permitting it to change and improve with time and experience. Ultimately, as you continue to work with the system, molding, customizing, and refining it to your personality, style, and requirements, it will become *your* approach. Some day it might occur to you to drop old Lyle Blessman a note of thanks for helping to steer you in the right direction. But basically YOU'RE the person you will have faith in and believe in, and over the long pull that's what counts the most.

Organize Your Time Like a Pro

"Time is money," Benjamin Franklin once said.

I would go a step further than that. Time is worth a whole lot more than money. If you lose money, you can recover it. You can earn back what you lost and more. You can't do that with time. Once time is gone, that's the end of it. You can't hoard time or reinvest it. You can't save it up "for a rainy day" the way you can with money. All you can do is spend it, and the way you spend it will determine how successful and happy you will be.

If you're in business, the way you plan and organize your time will in large measure influence the effectiveness of the way your business is operated, by yourself and by those who work with you. In my experience, this is true of any business and particularly true of the life insurance business. I've mentioned the old story that it takes some people a year to do a week's work and some people a week to do a year's work. I don't try to do a year's work in a week. But by the same token, I do my best to make sure I accomplish no less than a week's work in a week.

In no business that I know of is it easier to fritter away time than in the life insurance business. Some agents I have seen are experts in it, and that's one art in which I have no desire to be an expert. I make it my business to plan and organize my time like a professional for a variety of reasons. One is that I have yet to meet a true professional who doesn't value his time very highly, and anything worth valuing is certainly worth planning for. The second reason is that it makes my mind clearer and easier to know where I am going and what I am going to accomplish each day. Number three is that, as part of an organization, I owe it to my people to let them know where I am when they need me. And it goes without saying that I owe no less to my clients; I'm on call 24 hours a day and they know it. When you plan and organize your time, people know where you're at and you yourself know where you're at.

Finally, and this may be the most vital reason of all, I happen to be a dedicated family man. I have a lovely wife and four wonderful children and I have always wanted to be as successful with my family as I have been in the life insurance business. It will come as no surprise that the only way to succeed with your family is to spend time with your family. Doing that is very important to me and it helps me to balance my life.

I know that many businessmen *want and intend* to spend more time with their families. But a great number of them never actually get around to doing it, which is one of the reasons there's so much family strife and divorce in this country. Well, another thing I have learned is that the way to do with your time what you want and intend to do with it is to plan and organize your time on a regular day-to-day basis.

Anaylze Your Time Use. You may have heard the story of how famed advertising pioneer Ivy Lee, in a discussion with industrialist Charles Schwab some decades ago, was told by Schwab: "If you can show me a way to manage my time more effectively, I'll pay you anything within reason that you ask."

Lee responded by handing Schwab a blank sheet of paper. "Write down the six most important things you have to do tomorrow, and number them in their order of importance. Then take this paper out of your pocket in the morning and start working on number one and stick to it until it is done. Do the same thing with items two, three, four, and so on right down to the end of your list. Repeat the same thing every day. Don't worry how much you get done as long as you keep working on the most important tasks in their proper order of priority. After trying this system, if you are sold on its value, have your key people try it. If you feel it has been of any value to you, send me a check for what you think it is worth."

A few weeks later Lee received a check for $25,000. In those days $25,000 was worth more than $150,000 is today.

What had the businessman received for his money that he felt was so valuable? Lee, in less time than it would take you to shave or brush your teeth, had taught him the importance of planning his time. And of course the key to planning is analysis.

When was the last time you evaluated the way you utilize your time? If there's one thing I can say for a certainty, it's this: Whether you decide on The Blessman Approach or any other way of life you might prefer, you will apply it one helluva lot more effectively if you work periodic time analysis into the system. Analyzing the way you use your time today will make it easier for you to optimize the way you use your time in the future. At the same time it will help you to pinpoint things you are currently doing that result in squandered and unproductively used hours. As you probably know, any number of studies have been made of the way salesmen in a variety of industries use their time, and almost invariably the finding is that many salesmen waste as much as 50 or 60 percent of the selling hours they work and get paid for. And every so often you hear about this salesman or that salesman who learned how to analyze and organize his time more efficiently and doubled his productivity and earnings in the process, not to mention his self-esteem.

The question, of course—and this applies to your life both on and off the job—is: How can you tell if you are using your time effectively or not? This is fairly easy to assess once you get into the habit of doing it.

You use your time effectively when you:

* Achieve a stated objective.
* Help someone else achieve a stated objective.
* Work towards a stated objective.
* Make a friend.
* Improve yourself in some way.
* Do something beneficial for yourself or for somebody else.
* Enjoy yourself or give another person or persons enjoyment.

The trick is not to confuse nonproductive wasted time with the time you spend productively relaxing and enjoying yourself. Engaging in idle chatter or gossip, listening to a person who has nothing to say, viewing a TV program that bores you because you're too lazy or indifferent to turn it off, are some of the most popular ways to kill time. And they're not the ways to relax. In fact, doing nothing can make you nervous as hell.

Take a tip from the time management pro. Keep a running record of how you spend your time during a typical work week. It's fairly simple to do. Take a sheet of paper and divide each day's hours into fifteen minute segments. Then, after completing each task and each non-task, jot down in the appropriate space how the segments were spent. At the end of the week review your analysis record and pinpoint the useless and nonproductive segments. Repeat this exercise periodically, taking corrective measures each time. If you decide to tailor The Blessman Approach to your personal requirements, multiply the mileage you get out of the system by planning the time wasted out of your days, setting proper priorities, and performing tasks in their right order of importance to you.

The Plan Is the Thing. Very few people take the trouble to learn how to plan. They get inspirations that trigger good intentions, but let it stop there instead of converting the good intentions to action. Planning is a habit that requires the kind of imagination that enables you to sight ahead to fruition and the rewards of accomplishment.

I keep a planner that accounts for my time on a regular basis. Having developed this habit, I would find it hard to operate without it. The planner sits in my office for referral by members of my staff. They know where I'm supposed to be every hour of the day. They work with me to assure that I keep and don't confuse appointments inside or outside of the office with clients and other people, that I avoid conflicting commitments, and that I show up on time.

There are all kinds of time planning and scheduling aids and devices on the market, some of them costly and rather elaborate. But in my experience, planning needn't be sophisticated or complicated. Personnally, I'm a strong advocate of the shirt pocket planner. A consummate note writer, I carry pieces of paper around with me all the time, and since I know I rely on them I always keep them in the same place and they never get lost.

Whether it's on a memo pad sheet or on the back of an envelope, into my shirt pocket it goes. Someone once sent me a half dozen shirts without pockets and I sent them back. Shirts without pockets are like pencils without lead. When I undress for the night, the paper comes out of the pocket and goes onto the night stand. Next morning it goes back into the pocket of my shirt for the day. I refer to that paper a dozen times a day, adding items and crossing out things that I've already done. I number my things-to-do list in their order of priority, and that's how I work them out on a day-to-day basis.

There's nothing difficult or complicated about the system. It is simply a matter of habit. It's a habit I would strongly recommend, and if you feel this tip is worth $25,000, my address is Sterling, Colorado.

I don't think I could overstate the importance of writing things down, things-to-do as well as ideas. Developing a written plan and setting deadlines for each task not only keeps you on track, but conserves energy while it stimulates action. What if you run into the kind of task that is difficult or unpleasant to perform? When this happens I find it's a good idea, after writing it down, to tell others about it. Go on record. Put yourself on the spot. This spells out the goal on the one hand, establishes commitment on the other. If you default on the commitment, you lose face. Oriental or not, no one likes to lose face. Somehow, when you put yourself on record, the job seems to get done.

Never Forget Who the Boss Is

You've probably come across it yourself. Every so often you hear somebody say, "I'd like to go into business for myself."

Asked why, you get the standard reply: "I want to be my own boss."

Hey, don't let anyone kid you. These people are living in a dream world. I've been in business for myself for approximately two decades now, and I can tell you one thing for certain—*I am not my own boss.* In fact, I have several bosses: every one of my clients.

You are in business to serve others. If your service is helpful and beneficial, your customers or clients will be loyal. If it's not, they will seek other pastures. Your clients will make you or break you and there's no union you can complain to if an unhappy client decides to fire you. If you do decide to go into business for yourself, the best advice I can offer is: *Never forget who the boss is.* In all of my wanderings I have never met a successful businessman who does not share this philosophy.

A major U.S. corporation once spelled out for its employees "The Ten Commandments of Good Business." Among them:

* A CUSTOMER is not dependent on us ... we are dependent on him.

* A CUSTOMER is the most important person in any business.

* A CUSTOMER does us a favor when he calls—we are not doing him a favor by serving him.

* A CUSTOMER is a person who brings us his wants—it is our job to fill those wants.

* A CUSTOMER is the fellow that makes it possible to pay your salary whether you are a truck driver, plant employee, office employee, salesman, or manager. (Or, I might add, a life insurance agent.)

We live in an age of specialization where the main beneficiary is, or should be, the client. Some agents, however well meaning, tend to forget this simple fact of business life. In their desire to"close the order" they say things they don't mean and sometimes don't even understand to impress a prospective client or to frighten him into buying a policy.

From what I have seen, the use of pseudo-knowledgeability or scare tactics not only hurts the agent's credibility but undermines and deprofessionalizes the industry as well. I don't want to disturb people. I don't want to impress them. All I want is to serve them productively, to win their confidence and trust by means of proven dedication and action. If you take any other approach towards the person you work for—*your boss*—you are simply asking him to fire you.

Decide What You Want Out of Life

Is The Blessman Approach, or more correctly your personally tailored adaptation of The Blessman Approach, what you really want and need? It all depends on what you hope to get out of life.

To me it is very important to set personal as well as business goals for yourself. When I was first initiated into the insurance industry, as I discussed earlier in the book, I went through all of the harrowing, humiliating, and tortuous throes of trying to get established using the old time-worn conventional approach that any agent, novice or veteran, could imagine. I came to know call reluctance in its most agonizing forms. Wherever you have been, brother, I have been there before you. I have been through the wringer, wrenched, stretched, shrunk, and dried out. I tried the pitchman's packaged approach and I learned that when you practice hit-and-run salesmanship it's usually the agent who gets hit and the prospect who spends his time running from him.

In those early harrowing days I longed for self-repect and common dignity; to be treated as an equal by the successful businessmen I wanted to serve. I wanted their respect and admiration. I wanted them to have confidence in my ability and judgment and faith in my integrity and loyalty. These became my major objectives.

The Blessman Approach made all these aspirations come true.

Financial independence? I wanted that, too. I sure as hell did. I know what it means to try to raise a family on an inadequate income. I know how it feels to have the bills piling up while the savings account dwindles. As my business began to develop and success came my way, I appreciated the freedom from financial anxiety and all the wonderful things money could buy for myself and my loved ones—from airplanes and boats to that summer home in the country.

It is quite true that, as Henry Fielding once wrote, if you make money your god, it will plague you like the devil. But using The Blessman Approach, there's no chance of this happening because under this system of selling through service the financial success comes as a byproduct of your doing for others. And when it comes that way it is very easy to take and it doesn't go to your head.

It's a funny thing about money. Everyone wants it, yet very few will admit its importance to them. But I can tell you this: I haven't met a millionaire yet who complained about the hardships and evil of being rich. Usually the ones who knock money the hardest are the guys who can't make their ends meet. In my experience, when a person tells you money isn't worth working for, it probably means that he's broke.

In any case, that's another thing we ought to get clear in our minds. What's your main motivation? What's the spark that sets you on fire? Are you interested primarily in serving others or in serving yourself? Are you hooked on your personal ego or motivated primarily by the needs and desires of your clients? You can succeed either way if you're smart. But if you level with yourself it will make the process that much easier.

The route I have chosen, as I have said, will bring you personal and financial success as a byproduct of your service to others. Admittedly it is not the only way to make it. I know some agents who consistently write millions of dollars worth of business year in and year out who are largely driven by their own giant-sized egos. I admire these men and respect them. Still, whatever route we take, no matter now circuitous, in the end I believe we are all measured up against the same yardstick.

The point I'm getting at is this: The agents who are truly successful, the lofty Million Dollar Clubbers, whether driven by their own egos or not, are the professionals who are smart enough to recognize that the only way to serve yourself successfully is to serve others to their advantage and gain.

Maybe that's just another way of saying that they understand that their boss is the client.

Set Up a Target To Shoot At. Let's say you get out on the firing range. Your pistol is well oiled and in condition. You're stocked up on ammunition. You get into position to fire. And phfft! Nothing happens. You have nothing to shoot at. It's a point that nobody would argue —you would be wasting your time if you don't have a target to shoot at.

I don't know how many times I've said this already, but it bears repetition again and again. Without a target to shoot at you will have about as much chance at success as a guy in blue jeans applying for a bank president's job. I don't care if you sell life insurance, condominiums, or tooth brushes, market definition is your launching pad for success. The prospective clients have to be out there who have a desire and need for your product or service and the financial wherewithal to satisfy that need.

That's why my particular target is the prosperous businessman or professional. He needs what I am offering him. He has a set of financial problems and affairs that require analysis, definition, solutions, and integration. He's in desperate need of liquidity when estate reckoning time comes about. And he has the money to buy what he needs.

I learned very early in this business that calling on the factory or white collar worker who's in hock up to his scalp makes about as much sense as trying to squeeze a rock to get water out of it. This guy has no business or assets to protect; he has no estate worth discussing; and he couldn't afford what I'm selling even if he wanted it badly. I'm not putting him down. I can sympathize with this guy, but I can't do anything for him and he can't do anything for me. Yet he's the one thousands of agents keep calling on.

Okay, here's another $25,000 tip that won't cost you a cent. Whatever you wind up selling, whether it's life insurance or rugs, whether you use The Blessman Approach or some more brilliant approach you dreamed up for yourself, *start by defining your market.* If you use The Blessman Approach, don't bother. I've already done it for you. I have kept it no secret that the thing that keeps me going is that magic three out of four formula, the knowledge that 75 percent of all wealthy and successful businessmen and professionals don't have sufficient liquidity built into their estates, a gap that crucially needs to be plugged.

If you can beat that formula, brother, more power to you.

Believe In Yourself. The Blessman Approach will succeed for you in direct proportion to your ability to convince your prospective clients that you are honest, knowledgeable, sincere, and competent to help them solve their financial problems and fulfill their needs. Any agent worth his salt will tell you that the first and most essential step in making yourself believable to others is to believe in yourself.

Self-belief is mainly a matter of attitude. In this area life insurance salesmen have had a hard time of it over the years. I can tell you from personal experience that call reluctance is a chronic occupational hazard. The prospective client rarely summons the agent. Although the agent's and industry's image has risen in recent years, it isn't rising fast enough. Some agents I've run across are stage struck in Mr. Big's presence. Lacking total confidence in themselves, they feel the client doesn't respect them enough.

How can you combat this kind of negative thinking?

William James, considered by many to be the greatest American psychologist of this century, once said that "the greatest discovery of my generation is that human beings can alter their lives by altering their attitudes of mind."

One way to alter your attitude in a business where your mission is to help others straighten their financial affairs is to get your own affairs in order first. I think we have to examine our own personal situation and purchase cash value life insurance in the amount we can afford. Once we own it ourselves we will know first hand that life insurance is the finest and most secure property a person could own, the only property that will make other property hold its true value. Believing in and understanding the product you sell is one of the best strategies I know for strengthening your faith and belief in yourself.

Put All of Yourself Into Your Work

Halfway measures result in halfway careers. Andrew Carnegie once said that the average person puts only 25 percent of his energy and ability into his work.

Add that missing 75 percent to your career and you'll wind up miles ahead of competitors.

Start out by leveling with yourself. Subject your attitude, life, and career to stringent self-analysis. The more difficult the issue to face, the more you'll derive out of facing it. Honestly and openly assess the degree to which the following declarations apply to yourself.

True or false:

I lack confidence in my ability because I don't know enough about the product and service I sell.

I call mainly on marginal hard-to-sell candidates because I feel uncomfortable with the successful and prosperous businessman.

I'm not sufficiently believable because I use a canned sales pitch I don't believe in myself.

I sell life insurance as a stopgap career measure while I wait for a better paying more respectable job to become available.

Too many agents I know, if they leveled with themselves, would answer TRUE to too many of these statements. I ask you this: How can you make positive career inroads and progress when you start each day with such negative feelings?

The way to conquer a negative crippling attitude is through positive accomplishment. Don't agonize, organize. Organize your time; organize your approach; organize your thinking. *Organize uniqueness into your selling career!* Don't think "me too," think "me only." Most negative thinkers I know aren't making it because they blindly duplicate the unsuccessful techniques of others on a day-to-day basis.

The Blessman Approach is your password to opportunity's castle because it will help you stand out from Mr. Average Life Insurance Salesman if you apply yourself to the task with determination and diligence.

What undermines believability most? Lies. Deceit. Exaggerated statements and claims born out of desperation. Outmoded high pressure techniques. Lack of genuine knowledge and savvy. All the tactics and characteristics that helped to tarnish our potentially high level profession for years. The Blessman Approach has been designed to throttle these tactics and upgrade industry standards.

What creates and sustains client believability? Facts. Knowledge. The truth. Hard work. Sincerity grounded in integrity.

Ask any successful businessman you know: "Who's your accountant?", and he'll answer Bill Jones, or Joe Bailey.

Ask any successful businessman you know: "Who's your attorney?", and he'll answer Gable & Whitman, or Hawthorn Associates.

But ask him, "When was the last time your insurance agent called on you?", and he's apt to reply, "Well, Tom Wilson sold me a policy about three years ago . . . ."

Chances are the last time he saw his insurance man was the last time he bought a policy from him. Very few of us offer clients lifetime continuing service.

And if you asked that successful businessman, "Who's your financial coordinator?", chances are he'd respond with a blank expression.

And his expression wouldn't change if you asked him: "Who is helping you plan your estate? Who is handling your family gift program? Who sees to it that your wills and trusts are updated on a periodic basis as required? Who updates your business and financial planning in line with continuously changing legislation and tax requirements? Who helps you provide for the liquidity your estate will need to protect your business and assets? Who coordinates your business plans and goals with your family's personal aspirations and aims?''

The answer in at least three out of four cases will be nobody. Not a soul. His accountant isn't doing it; he's too busy with financial statements and tax work. His attorney isn't doing it; he's up to his eyebrows in routine legal matters.

So too often it just doesn't get done. *Somebody* ought to be doing it. It might just as well be you.

*   *   *

APPENDIX

ILLUSTRATIONS OF SETTLEMENTS COSTS
IN ESTATES OF $1,000,000

PEARCE C. RODEY
**Partner in Law Firm of Rodey, Dickason, Sloan, Akin & Robb,
Albuquerque, New Mexico**

SETTLEMENT COSTS

Gross Estate........$823.396	Debts...............$ 29,636
Total Costs.......... 255,597	Admin. Expense...... 1,581
	Executor's Fee....... 14,158
Net Estate.......... $567,799	N.M. Inheritance Tax . 10,187
Cash in estate, $13,673	*Federal Estate Tax .. 200,035
	TOTAL COSTS.....$255,597
	*No marital deduction

HAROLD HUBER
**Chairman, Hamilton Management Corp., Mutual Fund,
Denver, Colorado**

SETTLEMENT COSTS

Gross Estate.......$1,357,131	Debts...............$ 12,515
Total Costs........ 536,242	Notes Payable....... 138,418
	Admin. Expense...... 11,948
Net Estate......... $ 820,889	Attorney's Fee....... 60,000
Cash in estate, $40,847	Executor's Fee....... 50,000
	Colo. Inheritance Tax . 62,547
	*Federal Estate Tax .. 200,814
	TOTAL COSTS.....$536,242
	*$304,402 marital deduction

JOSEPH G. RICE
**President, First Federal Savings & Loan Association,
Phoenix, Arizona**

SETTLEMENT COSTS

*Gross Estate......$1,129,877	Debts...............$ 47,944
Total Costs........ 663,081	Notes Payable....... 224,103
	Admin. Expense...... 5,151
Net Estate......... $ 466,796	Accountant's Fee..... 3,300
*Includes $262,107 in separate	Attorney's Fee....... 12,000
property	Executor's Fee....... 23,000
Cash in estate, $9,749	Loss in sale of
	securities........ 239,919
Included in the gross estate is	Arizona State Tax.... 12,115
$75,190 of life insurance.	*Federal Estate Tax .. 95,549
	TOTAL COSTS.....$663,081
	*Full marital deduction.

EXHIBIT I

AVERAGE ESTATE CASH DEFICITS

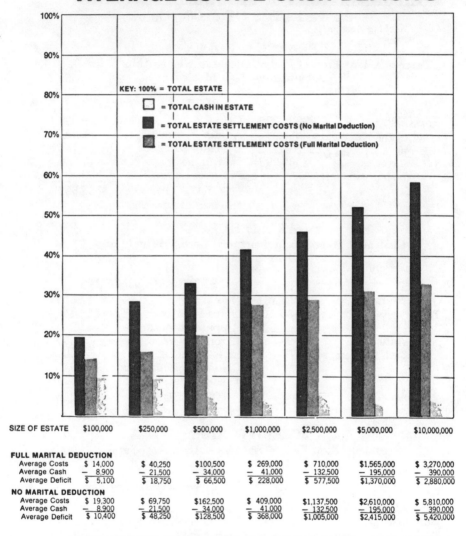

KEY: 100% = TOTAL ESTATE

☐ = TOTAL CASH IN ESTATE

◼ = TOTAL ESTATE SETTLEMENT COSTS (No Marital Deduction)

▨ = TOTAL ESTATE SETTLEMENT COSTS (Full Marital Deduction)

SIZE OF ESTATE	$100,000	$250,000	$500,000	$1,000,000	$2,500,000	$5,000,000	$10,000,000
FULL MARITAL DEDUCTION							
Average Costs	$ 14,000	$ 40,250	$100,500	$ 269,000	$ 710,000	$1,565,000	$ 3,270,000
Average Cash	− 8,900	− 21,500	− 34,000	− 41,000	− 132,500	− 195,000	− 390,000
Average Deficit	$ 5,100	$ 18,750	$ 66,500	$ 228,000	$ 577,500	$1,370,000	$ 2,880,000
NO MARITAL DEDUCTION							
Average Costs	$ 19,300	$ 69,750	$162,500	$ 409,000	$1,137,500	$2,610,000	$ 5,810,000
Average Cash	− 8,900	− 21,500	− 34,000	− 41,000	− 132,500	− 195,000	− 390,000
Average Deficit	$ 10,400	$ 48,250	$128,500	$ 368,000	$1,005,000	$2,415,000	$ 5,420,000

The findings appearing on this page were compiled by the Estate Research Institute, an independent statistical organization, from a survey of the court records of over 12,000 estates probated in all parts of the United States. The figures directly above reflect, in each estate size category, the average amount of estate settlement costs, the average amount of cash in the estate which was available to meet these costs, and the resulting cash deficit. The graph above these figures expresses in percentages the relation of the total estate to the costs to settle it, plus the cash available in the estate to meet these costs.

EXHIBIT I (Continued)

ASSET INVENTORY

1. *Cash Checking Account*............... $ 17,000 $ 17,000

2. *Real Estate*
   Ranch 640 A. @ $100 .... $ 64,000
   Snyder Ranch 1200 A. @ $110 132,000
   Home Place 309 Irrigated A. @ $1,500   463,000 - Joint Ownership
   Home .... 32,000 - Joint Ownership
   240 A. @ $75 18,000
   Wheat Land 1,280 A. @ $325 416,000
   Wheat Land 720 A. @ $300 216,000
   Elevator........................ 80,000

   Total: $1,389,500 .... $1,389,500

3. *Livestock*
   322 Cows @ $300................... $ 96,600
   290 Calves @ $120 34,800

   Total: $ 131,400 .... $ 131,400

4. *Machinery*
   All types farm .... $ 240,000
   Airplane....................... 75,000

   Total: $ 315,000 .... $ 315,000

5. *Outside Investments*
   XYZ, Inc........................ $ 60,000
   ABC, Inc....................... 90,000
   Acme Oil 45,000

   Total: $ 195,000 .... $ 195,000

6. *Stocks and Bonds*
   R. Stock 6,000 Shares @ $3.50 .... $ 21,000
   Energy Stocks
       A. Stock 7,400
       B. Stock 2,000
       C. Stock 1,800
       D. Stock 1,800

   Total: $ 34,000 .... $ 34,000

7. *Life Insurance Owners Life*
   Owned by Insured................. $ 151,500 .... $ 151,500

   Grand Total: $2,233,400

Indebtedness
   Federal Land Bank—Long-Term Loan $ 53,400
   Cattle Loans—Bank Note 65,000
   Operational Loan—Bank Note....... 115,000

   Total: $ 233,400 .... $ 233,400
   Total Net Worth: $2,000,000

EXHIBIT II

Suggestions & Recommendations

1. Review asset inventory and ownership conditions.
   A. Confirm valuations.

2. Review the jointly held property.

3. Discuss estate liquidity needs.
   A. Husband predeceases.
   B. Wife predeceases.

4. Discuss methods of meeting liquidity needs of estate.
   A. Borrow money.
   B. Sell property.
   C. Life insurance property owned and arranged.

5. Discuss possible use of gifts to reduce or equalize estate.
   A. Lifetime exemptions — $30,000.
   B. Annual exclusions — $3,000.

6. Determine the income-producing ability of net estate assets to wife and children.

7. Review wills and bring up to date.

8. Discussion of trusts and tax savings.

EXHIBIT III

Determination of Gross Estate, Death Taxes, Net Estate and Estate Liquidity

1. **Total Gross Estate** (Asset Inventory)		$2,233,400

To determine death taxes
Debts and expenses:

Debts (current bills and notes not deducted above)	$233,400	
Funeral and last expenses	11,500	
Administration Expenses (average for estate of similar size)	48,500	
2. **Total Debts and Expenses**		$ 293,400
3. **Adjusted Gross Estate** (Subtract Item 2 from Item 1)		$1,940,000

Deductions:

Marital Deduction (larger of $250,000 or one-half of Item 3)	970,000	
Charitable & Educational bequests	None	
4. **Total Deductions & Exemptions**		970,000
5. **Taxable Estate** (Subtract Item 4 from Item 3)		970,000

6. **Taxable Gifts** (Made After 12/31/76)		None	
Tentative Federal Tax on sum of Item 5 and Item 6		$334,100	
Minus: Tentative tax on Item 6		None	
Credit against Estate Tax		47,000	
State Death Tax credit		19,757	
7. **Federal Estate Tax Payable**		267,343	
8. **State Death Tax**		19,757	
9. **Total Death Taxes**			287,100

To determine net distributable estate

10. **Total Gross Estate** (Item 1)		$2,233,400
Total debts and expenses (Item 2)	$293,400	
Total death taxes (Item 9)	287,100	
11. **Total Debts, Expenses, and Death Taxes**		580,500
12. **Net Distributable Estate** (Subtract Item 11 from Item 10)		$1,652,900

To determine estate liquidity

13. **Total Debts, Expenses and Death Taxes** (Item 11)		$ 580,500
14. **General (Cash) Bequests**		None
15. **Total Cash Requirements** (Item 13 plus Item 14)		580,500
16. **Liquid Assets in Estate**		151,000
17. **Cash** (excess or deficit) for Estate Requirements (Item 16 minus Item 15)		429,500

EXHIBIT IV

Ledger Statement for ___Mr. Estate Owner___

Amount and Plan of Insurance $100,000
WHOLE LIFE

Annual Premium $ 3,177.00

[handwritten:] $2,500 Average premium
2,300 Average cash value
$ 200 Average Annual cos

DIVIDENDS USED TO REDUCE PREMIUMS
(PAYMENT IS THE ANNUAL PREMIUM LESS DIVIDEND)

End of Year	(1) Divi-dend*	(2) Pay-ment*	(3) Cash Value Incr.*	(4) Payment less C.V. Incr.*	(5) Cash Value	(6) Total Payments*	(7) Paid-Up Insur-ance	(8) Insur-ance*
1	300	2877	579	2298	579	2877	1200	100600
2	386	2791	2183	608	2762	5668	5600	101400
3	472	2705	2210	495	4972	8373	9900	102400
4	558	2619	2236	383	7208	10992	14100	103500
5	643	2534	2258	276	9466	13526	18100	104800
6	729	2448	2595	147CR	12061	15974	22500	106300
7	815	2362	2612	250CR	14673	18336	26800	107900
8	902	2275	2631	356CR	17304	20611	31000	109700
9	988	2189	2646	457CR	19950	22800	35000	111700
10	1075	2102	2661	559CR	22611	24902	38800	113800
11	1162	2015	2359	344CR	24970	26917	42000	116100
12	1250	1927	2369	442CR	27339	28844	45100	118500
13	1338	1839	2377	538CR	29716	30683	48100	121100
14	1427	1750	2381	631CR	32097	32433	50900	123800
15	1516	1661	2385	724CR	34482	34094	53700	126700
16	1592	1585	2386	801CR	36868	35679	56400	129800
17	1649	1528	2384	856CR	39252	37207	59000	132900
18	1707	1470	2383	913CR	41635	38677	61500	136200
19	1766	1411	2379	968CR	44014	40088	63900	139600
20	1826	1351	2373	1022CR	46387	41439	66200	143100

At Age				
60 →	34482	34094	53700	126700
65 →	46387	41439	66200	143100
**72 →	59966	47762	77300	173500

Premiums per $1,000

	Annual	Mo. I.S.A.†
Male Insur. #	31.67	2.72
Policy Fee	10.00	.86
Female Insur. #..	29.02	2.49
Waiver Premium..	.87	.08
Accidental Death..	.93	.08
Addn'l. Purchase..		

\# Add policy fee.
† Does not include service charge.
  Additional Benefits are Subject to
  Underwriting Limits.

At Age	Anl. Inc. Curr. IR▲	At Age
60 →	2755	60
65 →	4095	65
**72 →	6253	**72

29-0117 (50-100) (1974)   **NOT TO BE USED IN NEW YORK**

THE NORTHWESTERN MUTUAL LIFE
INSURANCE COMPANY · MILWAUKEE NML

Age   45 M

(handwritten: 2.5 %, 2.3 %, .2 % cost)

DIVIDENDS USED TO PURCHASE PAID-UP ADDITIONS
(PAYMENT IS THE ANNUAL PREMIUM)

(9) Cash Value Incr.*	(10) Payment less C.V. Incr.*	(11) Cash Value*	(12) Total Payments	(13) Paid-Up Insurance*	Values at Age 65 If Payments stopped	
					(14) Cash Value*	(15) Paid-Up Insurance*
879	2298	879	3177	1800		
2568	609	3447	6354	7000	7326	10465
2712	465	6159	9531	12300	12588	17983
2861	316	9020	12708	17600	17618	25168
2959	218	11979	15885	22900	22427	32037
3434	257CR	15413	19062	28800	27579	39398
3592	415CR	19005	22239	34700	32501	46429
3707	530CR	22712	25416	40700	37266	53236
3877	700CR	26589	28593	46700	41811	59729
4055	878CR	30644	31770	52600	46063	65803
3863	686CR	34507	34947	58100	49741	71056
4051	874CR	38558	38124	63600	53248	76066
4178	1001CR	42736	41301	69200	56676	80964
4370	1193CR	47106	44478	74700	59822	85457
4505	1328CR	51611	47655	80400	62979	89968
4689	1512CR	56300	50832	86200	66014	94303
4873	1696CR	61173	54009	91900	68835	98333
4947	1770CR	66120	57186	97700	71538	102194
5155	1978CR	71275	60363	103500	74046	105777
5294	2117CR	76569	63540	109300	76512	109300

Anl. Inc.
Curr. IR▲ *

		↓	↓	↓	Years to *:	
		51611	47655	.80400	PAY UP	19
		76569	63540	109300	ENDOW	25
4124		116929	85779	150800		
6759						
12193						

▲ *These Installment Refund income figures are based on current rates and are subject to change prior to the time payments begin.*

* *Based on current Dividend Scale. Not an estimate or guarantee of future results. First dividend contingent upon payment of second year premium.*

** *Life expectancy based on latest population statistics.*

Submitted by___Lyle L. Blessman___ Date_February 3, 19XX_

EXHIBIT V

INDEX